Peacock Bass Explosions!

Where, When & How To Catch America's Greatest Gamefish!

by Larry Larsen

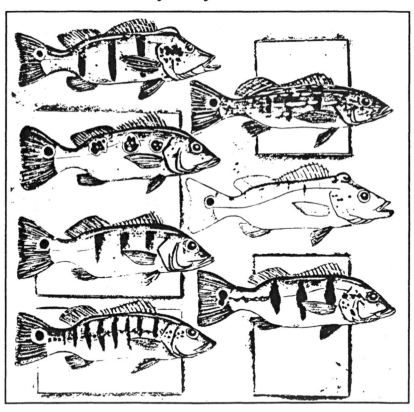

A LARSEN'S OUTDOOR PUBLISHING BOOK
THE ROWMAN & LITTLEFIELD PUBLISHING GROUP, INC.
Lanham • Chicago • New York • Toronto • Plymouth, UK

Published by
LARSEN'S OUTDOOR PUBLISHING
An imprint of The Rowman & Littlefield Publishing Group, Inc.
4501 Forbes Boulevard, Suite 200, Lanham, Maryland 20706
http://www.rlpgtrade.com

Estover Road, Plymouth PL6 7PY, United Kingdom

Distributed by National Book Network

British Library Cataloguing in Publication Information Available

Library of Congress Cataloging-in-Publication Data Available

Library of Congress 93-79801

ISBN: 978-0-936513-35-5 (paper: alk.paper)

♾™ The paper used in this publication meets the minimum
requirements of American National Standard for Information
Sciences—Permanence of Paper for Printed Library Materials,
ANSI/NISO Z39.48-1992.

Printed in the United States of America

LIBRARY ANNOTATION

Title: Peacock Bass Explosions

Author: Larry Larsen

Sports & Recreation
Fishing
799.1

ADULT SMALL PRESS
From a well-known outdoors journalist, "Peacock Bass Explosions" focuses on productive tactics that fool America's greatest gamefish, the peacock bass. It offers numerous tips on where, when and how to catch this exciting fish. Special features include detail information on Florida, Hawaii and fresh waters in the Caribbean, Central America and South America that harbor the fish.
192 pages Paperbound/

Table of Contents
Index
B&W Illustrations
Photographs

** Author Credentials **
He's America's most widely-read bass fishing writer and author. More than 1,500 of Larsen's articles have appeared in magazines, including Outdoor Life, Sports Afield, and Field & Stream. Larsen has authored 15 books on bass fishing and contributed chapters to another eight.

Part 2. Preparing For Action

The avid bass angler for 35 years has caught and released hundreds of peacock bass between five and 21 pounds. Larry Larsen has traveled the globe to fish for peacocks, including stops in South Florida, Brazil, Venezuela, Panama and Hawaii. He is a four-time (currently) world record holder on the peacock bass. Larsen was awarded four line class world records in 1993 for Peacock Bass (Cichla spp) by the National Fresh Water Fishing Hall of Fame in Hayward, WI. The records for the four peacock bass, which weighed up to 20 pounds, were established in the 14, 16, 20 and unlimited pound line classes.

ABOUT THE AUTHOR

Larry Larsen is America's most widely read bass fishing writer and author and the first to pen a book on peacock bass. He is a frequent contributor on both largemouth and peacock bass subjects to major outdoor magazines. More than 1,500 of Larsen's articles have appeared in magazines, including Outdoor Life, Sports Afield, Field & Stream, Bassin', North American Fisherman, Bass Fishing, Fishing Facts and Fishing Tackle Trade News. His photography has appeared on the covers of many national publications.

The Lakeland, Florida outdoor writer/photographer has now authored 15 books on bass fishing and contributed chapters to another eight. They include the award-winning BASS SERIES LIBRARY, GUIDE TO FLORIDA BASS WATERS SERIES and others. He has also authored books on fishing opportunities in the Caribbean.

The Lakeland, FL based author is President of Larsen's Outdoor Publishing (LOP), the fastest growing publisher of outdoor titles in the country, and a member of the Outdoor Writers Association of America (OWAA), the Southeastern Outdoor Press Association (SEOPA), and the Florida Outdoor Writers Association (FOWA). Complete information on the author's other books and the LOP line of outdoor books can be found in the Resource Directory at the back of this book.

The author is not just a writer who has studied and written about all aspects of bass fishing for more than 23 years and peacock bass fishing for five years, he is an accomplished angler. As a result, his published works detail proven fish catching methods and special techniques. Larry works with several tackle companies on new lure and techniques development. His analysis of what works and why will help anyone catch more and bigger fish!

INTRODUCTION
THE PEACOCK - IN YOUR FACE!

The peacock bass by nature is aggressive and its personality is downright belligerent. It is a fish so powerful that it can destroy tackle, straighten hooks and tear the hardware right out of hardwood and plastic baits. The fiercest fighting fish in the world will smash and mangle lures, even break them apart, and then give you the battle of your life.

It is impossible to exaggerate the strike and fight of this colorful gamefish. The larger it gets, in contra-distinction to its North American cousins, the better it fights. The fish almost always jumps the second they are hooked, and after a head-shaking leap or two, they make an incredible run. Even a four- or five-pounder can wear a person out, and they probably grow to over 30 pounds!

In a long, straight run, the aerial acrobat weighing over 15 pounds can rip 40-pound test line from a heavy-duty 3:1 ratio casting reel with the drag clamped down tight. The trophy-size peacock can easily break 20- to 30-pound test monofilament or straighten out a 3X heavy-strength hook in one of its initial charges or when it sees the boat and senses doom.

What makes an angler whose favorite fish is the musky, smallmouth bass, striper, or giant largemouth dream of another species? What would make a snook or tarpon guide give up on them to chase after a freshwater species? It's the fish that is head and shoulders above all the others in this world: the peacock bass. Imagine a 12-Megaton hydrogen bomb going off below your topwater plug or giant popper.

There is no such thing as a pot-bellied peacock bass. Pound for pound, the peacock is the toughest-fighting freshwater gamefish in the world!

There is no such thing as a pot-bellied peacock bass. Its splashy colors make it virtually impossible to sneak up on its forage, so if it can't catch the food, a peacock goes hungry. As a result, a giant peacock is just as quick as a smaller fish ... and a lot more powerful.

The fighting ability of the peacock puts them at the head of the class. Pound for pound, it is the toughest-fighting freshwater gamefish in the world With the exception of the tuna family, the peacock bass, I believe, is the top battler in global waters of any salinity. When you consider the jumping ability, the power, the attitude and the excitement generated by large peacock bass, no other fish even comes close.

Peacocks love topwater lures; they love TO DESTROY them!

Their Deadly Range

These fish originate and thrive in the same South American waters of two dreaded species: the piranha and the powerful payara. The blood-hungry piranha grow to five or six pounds and the devilish saber-toothed payara maxs out at over 30. Any fish that can hold its own where these and other hellacious predators live has to be tough. Peacock bass are among the 1,800 other species that have been cataloged from the Amazon home waters.

Fortunately, the range of the peacock bass has grown substantially. Today, you can fish for them in three places - Florida, Hawaii and Puerto Rico - without even needing a passport. The fish can be found in Panama, and I'm told by good authority, Costa Rica in Central America. The biggest of these bruisers, though, still live in South America. Venezuela, Brazil and Colombia harbor the most giant peacocks, and other countries, such as Guyana, Suriname, French Guiana, Ecuador, Peru and Bolivia, have waters that contribute to the massive Amazon watershed which abounds with peacock bass.

What the Peacock Is and Isn't

The peacock is not really a "bass" at all. The two fish similar in stature and sporting qualities are genetically far apart. The peacock, which has attained documented weights in excess of 26 pounds, is called bass because it strongly resembles a largemouth in general size and shape. However, it is actually the largest American member of the cichlid family of fishes which also includes the guapote ("rainbow bass"), oscar, and tilapia, among many others.

The cichlid family, with 1,400 species in the world and 250 to 300 in South America, is to tropical waters as the sunfish family, which includes the black basses, is to temperate freshwaters of North America. Some biologists believe that the two were derived from a common ancestor, a prehistoric saltwater perch.

The IGFA and National Fresh Water Fishing Hall of Fame do recognize the fish under the common name of peacock bass, but the peacock is more commonly called "pavon" in Spanish-speaking countries and "tucunare" in Brazil and Hawaii.

General Description

Once you see the fish, you'll understand why it is called a peacock bass by most North Americans. The peacock bass derives its name from the large conspicuous, ocellated (ringed in gold) black mark on its tail, which resembles the vivid "eye" on the beautiful plume of a peacock's tail. Hence the name, "peacock bass." The distinctive gold-embroidered circular black halo spot on all peacock bass tails reminds some more of the savage eye of a jungle cat.

The prominent "false eye" on the tail is actually a deceptive target for predators. Most all fish have a black eye on their heads, and

*S*everal species within the genus Cichla are commonly referred to as peacock bass. Exactly how many species of the colorful peacock there really are depends on which biologist you speak with.

some have evolved physically one or two ways to "misguide" an attack to the eye area from predators. One common evolution is the eye spot near the rear of the fish. Another is color patterns that obscure the eye or detract from its prominence. The peacock bass has both a false eye on the tail, and vivid and irregular color patterns on the head.

The rainbow-like coloration of the peacock bass is striking; the colors rival many saltwater coral reef fish. It generally has a dark greenish-black or bronze back and a light white belly with rear underside that ranges from golden to mellow yellow or light chartreuse to pink or blood red. It normally has a main body background area of green, yellow, burnished gold or dark black hues and irregular broad and dusky black vertical bars along its sides.

Gill covers, tail and fins on the lower half of the body (pelvic and anal fins) are subtly-splashed with traces of hues that widely vary from bronze to bright orange to pink to crimson red to a greenish yellow. The pectoral fins are not colored. Colors on the lower gill plate, however, can be vivid. Black splotches (patterned like random ink spots) abound on the gill covers (near the eye) of the speckled peacock. Dorsal fins may be a translucent aquamarine or bluish-gray, as can be the top half of the tail fin.

Add to the above their always striking scarlet or blood red (iris) eyes that stare you down when the fish is mad as hell at you, and you will have the complete picture, as words can describe such.

During spawning season and when the fish are disturbed or actively feeding, color may intensify, and breeding males (and some females as well, according to the latest scientific reports) develop a prominent hump on their forehead. In darker, stained waters, such as Venezuela's Casiquiare and Orinoco Rivers, the peacocks are extremely colorful. In clear waters, like Venezuela's Lake Guri, or the South Florida canals, the peacocks are more pale in coloration. Like most black bass in the states, the water has a lot to do with their coloration.

Peacock bass also have a single nostril, spines in the dorsal, anal and pelvic fins, and a solid row of short, sharp teeth that can cut through heavy monofilament line relatively easily. Steel leaders, contrary to some advisors, are not necessary. However, the teeth make handling of large peacocks difficult without the aid of a glove or grip-pliers.

Let's Play The Name Game

Several species within the genus *Cichla* are commonly referred to as peacock bass. Some biologists, literature and/or tour operators contend that there are five distinct species of the colorful peacock, others three or four, and still others say there could be, in fact, a dozen species. One biologist, in fact, reportedly claims there are perhaps two dozen species of peacock. Exactly how many species of the colorful peacock there really are depends on which biologist you speak with.

Today, the International Game Fish Association (IGFA) lists two "with several other variants that may prove to be valid species as well." According to existing scientific literature from many English-speaking fishery biologists, there are currently three different species of peacock bass. Kirk Winemiller, of the Dept. of Wildlife and Fisheries Sciences at Texas A&M University's College of Agriculture and Life Sciences describes five in Venezuela. Sven Kullander of the Swedish Royal Museum is currently completing a paper that identifies a dozen or so.

Few will deny that the fishery community currently doesn't have a good handle on the taxonomic identification - number and change of species. And, the peacocks apparently do go through appearance changes.

"In our study ponds, we had several one- to two-pound speckled peacock with bold speckled patterns the spring of 1984," says Florida biologist Paul Shafland. "Just five months later, they had changed so dramatically we thought that we were in the wrong pond. We started to observe them carefully after that and establish more confirmation of the changes they go through."

Most species of peacocks, especially the two in the Florida canal system, change appearance with age, except for the tail spot. The fact that these species change so much hasn't made it easy for biologists, let alone layman anglers.

The confusion between biologists regarding the number of species is not without precedent. Southeastern fisheries agencies and biologists still argue about whether the "Shoal bass" is a true species of black bass or a subspecies (distinctive race related to) of the redeye bass. They may never agree on that, and we may never know for sure about peacock bass, since their native range is far away from easy access to the most experienced (generally) and advanced community of biologists.

The common English name, peacock bass, is derived by Americans from the common Spanish name, "pavon" (which means peacock). "Pavon" is derived from "pavo real." In Venezuela, the pavon is the national freshwater fish of the country. The fish is also called "tucunare" (from a Tupi Indian/Portuguese dialect, pronounced "too-coon-array") in Brazilian, Panamanian and Hawaiian waters, and "lukanani" in Guyana waters.

Species Identification

The butterfly peacock or *Cichla ocellaris* (also called mariposa pavon, estrella (star) pavon, amarillo (yellow), marichapa and sargento) is a typically yellow-green fish with three black rosette (circular) markings on each side along the lateral line at an early stage of life. As it grows older and larger (generally at one to two pounds), most of the fish develop three black vertical bars which substitute for the haloed spots on each side.

The bars or circular markings then begin to fade in some peacocks. Some biologists have claimed that the bars on a sexually mature fish are reduced in length and appear as the three large circular black spots during breeding. One fishery expert has described a similar species with three bars that are wedge shaped, being wider at the top than at the bottom. For the biologist out there, there are 80 to 95 scales along the butterfly's lateral line.

Fish over four pounds normally retain their base coloration which may vary from green to gold, depending on the water they come out of, the time of the year and perhaps other factors. The butterfly, which reaches about 12 pounds in South America, is the primary fish stocked in South Florida canals, Panama and Hawaii. This species is not as much of a surface feeder as the speckled or grande peacock.

The butterfly peacock is a typically yellow-green fish with three black circular markings on each side along the lateral line at an early stage of life. As the peacock grows to one to two pounds, many of the fish develop three black vertical bars which substitute for the haloed spots on each side.

The butterfly does, however, have the most extensive range of all peacocks. It is also generally more abundant than other peacocks in a waterway that contains more than one specie of them.

Some biologists believe that the butterfly is also the fish called *Cichla orinocensis.* Others, like Winemiller, call it a separate species, the main descriptive difference being that the *c.ocellaris* has more irregular rosettes on each side and yellow (versus orange) anal fins. Winemiller cites different South American ranges for the two.

The speckled peacock has prominent horizontal row markings along the flanks that take the form of a white or yellowish dot and/or dash pattern.

"*C. orinocensis* occurs in the Orinoco and Amazon River drainages, except it may be replaced by *C. ocellaris* in northeastern Amazonas and *C. monoculus* in western and southern Amazonas," he says. "*C. ocellaris* occurs in the Essequibo River drainage in Guyana and easternmost Venezuela. It possibly may occur in northeastern Amazonas as well."

The speckled peacock, or *Cichla temensis* (also called spotted, pintado, trucha, tigre (tiger), pinta de lapa, venado (deer) and cinchado), is defined by black blotches on its gray-hued cheek plates. The butterfly and royal peacocks do not have the marking. The cheek blotches are also the only identification parameter that is consistent between a large speckled peacock and a smaller one. It too, is the basis for the belief of some biologists that the speckled and the "grande pavon" are the same species.

The fish we'll call speckled has prominent horizontal row markings along the flanks that take the form of a white or yellowish dot and/or dash pattern. The speckled peacock starts life with a dark olive green to purple color and two to six bold, interrupted lines. (For the biologists out there, there are 100 to 120 scales along the lateral line.) The speckled peacock as described here can reach about 15 to 18 pounds, although specimens over 10 are rare.

The speckled with the dash pattern along their sides seem to inhabit waters with a little more current than do larger members of this species (or other species). Consequently, they are found more frequently along river banks than are what many call the "grande

*M*any fisheries biologists believe the grande peacock is the same species as the speckled peacock. The grande peacock prefer the quieter waters of lagoons and lakes off rivers. They are the biggest of all peacocks and grow to over 30 pounds is South American waters. Most of the pictures in magazines and books showing peacocks weighing over 12 pounds are of this fish. The average size of most grande peacocks is around three or four pounds, but several between six and eight pounds may be taken on a typical day in many areas. Some areas produce monsters over 10 pounds on a fairly regular basis.

peacock'' or ''peacock pavon''. Some have reported the peacocks with the specks to be the best fighter of all. I can attest that they certainly perform with very high standards.

Winemiller contends that the speckled with prominent white spots running horizontally is a non-breeding female *C. Temensis*. He believes that the faint black vertical bars intensify in a spawning female and that a non-breeding male resembles the non-breeding females except for two things. The non-breeding male's cheek pigment is less prominent and the white spots tend to fade.

One reference source describes a peacock, probably a speckled, as having three faint bars and heavy spotting on the pectoral, ventral and tail fins. They called this fish a ''spot-fin pavon.'' The speckled peacocks, which are said to lose their side dot and dash patterns in

T he "royal" peacock is a dark green to golden brown peacock with an irregular black band which runs laterally along each grayish side all the way to the tail "eye."

later years, exhibit spots on their upper fins. The fish has been introduced into South Florida canals.

The grande peacock, (also called grande pavon and peacock pavon) is thought to be, by Shafland, Winemiller and many other fisheries biologists, the same species as the speckled peacock or *Cichla temensis* described above. Other biologists disagree and call it a separate species. Winemiller describes this fish, sans prominent white lateral spots, as a male-breeding *Cichla temensis*. The grande peacock (I'll call it that for distinction here) has the three very prominent black vertical bars and prominent cheek blotches.

The "royal" peacock, or *Cichla intermedia* (also called *C. nigrolineatus* by some while others believe the name is invalid) (also called the black striped peacock) is a dark green to golden brown peacock with an irregular black band which runs laterally along each grayish side all the way to the tail "eye." It is crossed intermittently and less conspicuously by seven to nine faint black transverse stripes (thin bars), instead of three prominent bars. In juveniles, the black band usually with yellow borders is continuous, but larger specimens may have a discontinuous band and interrupted lateral line on one side or the other.

There are 80 to 95 scales along the lateral line of this fish which prefers clear rivers with slow-moving current. Seldom will the fish weigh over 10 pounds. Its distribution to date is limited to the Orinoco watershed in Venezuela south of San Fernando. That

COMMON NAMES IN THE PEACOCK RANGE			
SPECIES	Florida	Venezuela	Brazil
Family Nm	Peacock	Pavon	Tucunare
Scientific Name			
1. *C. ocellaris* (*C. orinocensis*)	butterfly	mariposa amarillo marichapa estrella	-acu, -assu -comum
2. *C. temensis*	speckled	tigre, trucha venado pinta de lapa spotted	-tinga, -branco
3. *C. temensis*	(grande) speckled	grande pavon cinchado pintado	-paca
4. *C. intermedia* (*C. nigrolineatus*)	royal (black-striped)	royal pavon real	
5. *C. monoculus*	gray-bar	–	gray bar five bar

Note: In Hawaii, the common name for this species is tucunare. In Panama, they call it tucunare or sargento, and in Puerto Rico, as well as it other Spanish-speaking countries in South America, it's the pavon. In Guyana, they call it the lukanani. In all areas, it is usually also known as the peacock bass.

includes the rivers Casiquiare, Cinaruco and Capanaparo. The royal peacock has not been stocked out of its native range.

The "gray-bar" peacock, or *Cichla monoculus* (also called the five-bar or Rio Das Mortes tucunare) is a light olive gray peacock with five faint black (gray) vertical bars on its sides, instead of three dark black vertical bars. Brazilian experts believe this Rio Das Mortes peacock to be limited in distribution primarily to the translated "River of Death" (Rio Das Mortes) watershed in southern Brazil. Others contend the range could well extend from Peru to southeastern Brazil and north to the Casiquiari watershed.

The bars on the *C. monoculus* peacock, according to fisheries biologist Winemiller, may appear as triangular in shape. A few black cheek spots are present on this species.

The "gray-bar" peacock is light olive gray with five faint black (gray) vertical bars on its sides, instead of three dark black vertical bars.

Other Peacock Species or Subspecies

Some literature describes additional species within the genus and offers common names but no scientific names. Other technical papers describe taxonomic relationships of similar fish and offer a scientific name without a current common moniker.

Another such peacock is the *Cichla chacoensis* (scientific name) whose range is reportedly the Rio Parana and La Plata region of Argentina, Uruguay and Paraguay. Very little else is known about this fish or described in literature. Another species called *Cichla atabapensis* is considered identical to *C. ocellaris*.

Brazilian biologists suggest there may be as many as seven very similar but distinguishable species of Cichla. Venezuela biologists believe there may be four or five and some fisheries biologist have identified up to two dozen species based on both geographic and trait definitions.

In the scientific community, there currently exists philosophical differences on what defines strains, sub-species or variants among the cichla family. The nomenclature is currently in flux and will probably continue to be so for awhile. Ultimately, it will not surprise me if the number of species of peacock bass ended up somewhere midway between three and 11.

Dissimilarities To Love

The fish are similar to largemouth in many ways. They have similar habits and habitat preferences and are caught on similar

I n the scientific community, there exist philosophical differences on what defines strains, sub-species or variants among the cichla family.

lures. The ways they are less similar makes them even more exciting. They are tougher, meaner and slightly bigger. They feed only during daylight hours. As a schooler, peacocks are more like the saltwater dolphin.

Most fish roam in schools, but the peacock bass is known for roaming in gangs. The peacock bass is something of a thug. A hooked fish triggers the others in the school to search and destroy prey of their own. Leaving a hooked fish in the water until a second one nearby is hooked will prolong the excitement.

I call it the ''World's Greatest Gamefish'' because it is attracted to cover, strikes topwater lures regularly, jumps when hooked, never gives up a battle, is powerful enough to tax angler skills and tackle, breaks line and lures easily, has a physical appearance that looks exciting, and obtains an average size of 15 to 25 pounds (a very respectable weight).

I must warn anglers that they will not land all the peacocks that they hook. ''You'll need a well rope and a winch to get one in,'' an avid peacock bassman once stated. ''You'll need saltwater gear, surf rods and such, because conventional tackle just won't hold them.''

Fortunately that opinion isn't true for a relatively knowledgeable angler, but it does takes a certain level of skill to handle these fish. They can bring the macho musky angler to his knees. They can twist the world-class tarpon angler into a pretzel, and they can give striped bass and smallmouth bass fishermen a bird's nest cocoon that will handcuff them.

''I've caught angry 100-pound tarpon that didn't blast a plug as hard as peacock bass do,'' said Biff Lampton, Editor of Florida Sportsman magazine. Other expert anglers have made similar observations.

I have seen a couple of so-called ''professional'' tournament anglers literally crying in their beer after several days of trying to successfully battle peacocks. I have seen editors of ''big-time'' magazines hit shore with only mangled tackle and nerves to show for their morning's efforts.

And, I have seen the smiles on many faces when everything goes right, and the angler lands the most exciting fish of his life - a giant peacock bass!

Chapter 1

GOLDEN BASS OF FLORIDA'S GOLD COAST

Over 1,000 miles of freshwater canals

We weren't in some exotic country overseas. The large birds in the overhanging trees weren't colorful South American macaws; they were birds of prey. The "mountain" to the south of us was a landfill embankment, yet my wife, Lilliam and I were enjoying some very exciting action on peacock bass.

The canal waters that we were fishing were clear, as opposed to the tannic-stained waters in the jungles of South America, but the fish we were seeking was the same. It had an inherent desire to be aggressive, mean, and high-flying. The golden bass of Southeast Florida are relatively new transplants, but they are going to make their mark.

Lilliam's first battle with an American peacock was similar to several she and I had with those in Venezuela several months earlier. The fish hit with a vengeance and jumped five times before she pulled it aboard.   The shiner free-lined behind the slowly-moving boat didn't have a chance, but neither did the next three set out by her and our fishing partner, Paul Shafland.

Shafland, a biologist with the Florida Game and Fresh Water Fish Commission, and not coincidentally the director of their Non-Native Fish Research Laboratory, had kindly consented to show us a part of the South Florida canal system and the booming fishery that he and his counterparts have developed. After four feisty peacocks of one to two pounds caught and released in less than an hour, we were quickly impressed.

P aul Shafland, Director of the Non-Native Fish Research Laboratory for the Florida Game & Fresh Water Fish Commission, has helped create a booming fishery in the South Florida canal system.

While Paul and Lilliam closely watched over shiners set out behind the boat, I worked a topwater plug along the canal's sharp drop. The lure that had accounted for about 20 peacock bass per day per person on our first trip to Venezuela resulted in nothing for me that morning. It wasn't until I changed to a white jig that I caught my first peacock from the 100-foot wide canal. In a little over two hours that morning, we caught and released about 10 of the battling peacocks.

Florida Limits

Retaining a fiercely fighting peacock bass is legal. The Florida peacock bass season opened on all state waters in July of 1989, but

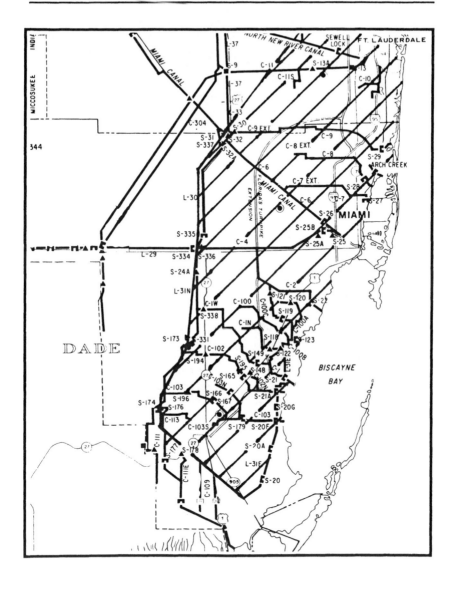

their distribution is limited to fresh waters in the southeastern part
of the state, primarily in Dade and Broward counties. The daily bag
limit on butterfly peacock bass is two, only one of which can be
greater than 17 inches. The speckled peacock is completely protected
and is a catch-and-release fish only.

"Our purpose is to protect the larger fish, more so than the
smaller ones," says Shafland. "The limit gives those that catch a
wall-hanger a chance to mount it and also allows those that want to
eat a couple to do so. We also want to strongly encourage catch and
release. Although it's legal, we wouldn't like to see someone going
out every day and keeping a limit."

The entire coastal canal system in Southeast Florida is
interconnected, so the range of the brightly-colored peacock bass is
throughout them all. Once they were introduced, the population
exploded, spreading rapidly through endless miles of waterways that
wind under bridges and through the backyards of housing
developments and shopping centers.

Primary Study Area

The commission's primary study area is about 70 miles long by
35 miles wide, and while that seems small, there is plenty of water to
fish. The system encompasses well over a 1,000 miles of interconnected
canals, according to Shafland. Peacock bass swim in all of it.

The waterways are interconnected but navigation from one to
another is limited due to water control structures every 10 miles or
so. Some areas offer excellent ramps for very large water craft, while
in other canals, a johnboat dropped in from shore is best suited for
enjoying the experience.

The canals range from very small with difficult access to larger
systems with concrete ramps. Canals intersect each other periodically
on all systems, and some run into or through small lakes, such as
those near the Miami International Airport.

Miami Canal Aesthetics

Many canals are tiny with limited access, while other larger
systems accommodate up to 300 man-hours per acre of angling
pressure, according to Shafland. Most canals have noisy bridges
overhead, but you will normally fish without competition. As more
fishermen begin to find out about this great bass, their popularity will
continue to grow and that will change.

Some of the canals around Miami are not located in the best of
neighborhoods, so get local advice regarding launching sites. The

clear water allows you to watch assorted exotic fishes swimming among the strange--and sad--repository for shopping carts, bicycles and other scattered litter on the bottom. Aesthetically, the endless miles of drainage canals in South Florida are not pristine waterways. They have been drastically urbanized by development.

While some of the canals are aesthetically unpleasant, many are relatively clean with water visibility down to 15 feet. Most are uniformly 13 to 15 feet deep starting very near the shoreline. They all have an overabundance of forage, primarily exotic forage species, and that fact, plus historical information of the temperatures of the canal system, led to the development of the peacock bass study.

Prime Dade/Broward Areas

Several canals along the so-called Gold Coast area have potential value for such recreation, currently largely ignored. The Mowry Canal in South Dade County and Snake Creek at the Dade-Broward County line are just a couple of waterways with excellent peacock bass fishing. Some others without names are even better.

Shafland notes that many of the better areas are found between the C-103 Canal at Homestead north to Snake Creek. Some small lakes connecting with the canal system offer good peacock bass fishing as well. The lakes near the Miami International Airport are good examples.

The Tamiami Canal (C-4) Airport Lakes system consists of Blue Lagoon Lake and Lake Mahar, among others. Both are excellent peacock spots. The Maceo Park boat ramp off NW 7th Street provides access to the system at Blue Lagoon. You'll find the area near the launch is designated a manatee zone, so slow boat speeds are necessary.

The shallows and shoreline of Blue Lagoon are productive early in the day. On the northern side of the lake is an area full of submerged debris, such as trees and barges, that is called the "Sunken Forest." The area all along the Dolphin Expressway (Route 836) shoreline is very productive for peacock bass.

Lake Mahar, also called "Second Lake" is located about a mile west of Blue Lagoon along the canal. It offers good action early and late in the day along a residential shoreline on the southern end and along the shallow obstructions on the western side. Tiny Hidden Lake lies further west along C-4 and harbors numerous peacocks as well. So do several side canals with docks, piers and bridges off the Tamiami Canal.

Most major canal systems around Miami and Homestead have been stocked. Farther north, peacocks are also thriving in the C-14

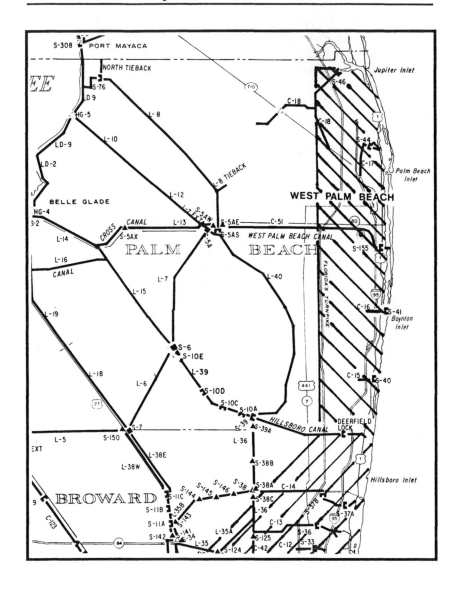

Canal near Fort Lauderdale and Pompano Beach and, to the west, the series of canals converging near the Tamiami Trail have also received peacocks. Peacocks seem to be scattered everywhere in the canal system but may be concentrated in certain areas.

Shafland's choice of the top canal systems, for those who want to use a map to search out prime peacock waters, include the following waterways:

1. Mowry Canal (C-103)	8. Miami Canal (C-6)
2. Princeton (C-102)	9. Biscayne Canal (C-8)
3. Black Creek (C-1)	10. Snake Creek (C-9)
4. the C-100 series	11. South New River (C-11)
5. Snapper Creek (C-2)	12. North New River
6. Tamiami Canal (C-4)	13. Middle River (C-13)
7. Airport Lakes area	14. Pompano Canal (C-14)

All contain fishable butterfly peacock bass populations, according to the biologist responsible for the peacock program.

Distribution North

While the primary fishery lies between Canal S-20 south of Miami and the Hillsboro Canal west of Deerfield Lock, a limited peacock fishery exists between the Florida Turnpike and the intracoastal north to Jupiter Inlet. The future expansion of the peacock's range along Florida's east coast will probably be sporadic populations depending on the severity of the winters in the state.

The great thing about this fishing is that you don't even have to know the name of the canal that you are fishing. For more information on the exotic fishery of Florida, contact: Paul Shafland, Director, Non-Native Fish Research Laboratory, Florida Game and Fresh Water Fish Commission, 801 N.W. 40th St., Boca Raton, FL 33431 or phone (407) 391-6409.

Early State Records Fall

Florida's newest fishery continues to spawn state records. Ever since the season was opened on peacock bass, anglers in South Florida have focused on setting a lasting record. None have succeeded to date. Most of the record fish have been caught from different canals, indicating butterfly peacocks are growing well throughout the coastal canal system.

On July 1, 1989, peacock bass were given official gamefish status in Florida. The first official state record butterfly peacock, caught by a Fort Lauderdale angler in November of 1990, weighed 5.36 pounds, but this record was broken less than five months later. The first state record peacock was caught in the Bel Aire Canal in Dade County.

T his Florida record is one of many state marks set over the past few years.

Mark Soucy caught the peacock from the popular honey hole by fishing a nightcrawler threaded on a tiny number 8 hook.

The second state record butterfly peacock bass was caught in April of 1991 by Jed Drucker while fishing Snake Creek (C-9). The 26-year old angler from Pembroke Pines caught the fish on a jig and tube bait and 6 pound test line. His 6 pound, 7 1/4 ounce peacock established another short-lived Florida mark. Drucker's fish measured 21 1/2 inches in length and had a 16 1/4-inch girth.

The angler had planned on releasing the fish back into the same waters from which it was removed, but unfortunately, it died. Drucker kept the fish alive for more than 24 hours by aerating and regularly changing the water in his tank.

Drucker's mark didn't last long. On August 3, 1991, a new record weighing 6 pounds, 13 ounces and measuring 21.1 inches in length and 16 inches in girth was caught by Miamian George Walker using live bait while fishing in Snapper Creek (C-2). Walker froze the fish prior to weighing it on certified scales and having it inspected by a Commission biologist.

Incidentally, the Snapper Creek Canal off Miller Road is one of the area's hottest peacock spots, according to Charlie Boxmeyer of the Sea Shack Tackle and Bait shop in West Kendall. Many of the peacock fishermen use large wild shiners which are extremely productive there.

Nelson Gardner of Naranja caught another big butterfly peacock on February 19, 1990, using a blue and silver Rat-L-Trap. Believing it too small for a record, put it in his freezer to await a trip to the taxidermist. He weighed it in on certified scales for entering the

There are plans to increase the stocking rate of the larger-growing speckled peacock into the South Florida canal system at a future date.

Metropolitan South Florida Fishing Tournament (MET). The fish weighed 7 pounds, 6 ounces.

Over a year later, his father was reading the paper and noticed a story about Drucker catching a smaller state record peacock. The 16-year old Nelson and his father realized then that they had a larger fish in their freezer. A phone call to a biologist assured him that the fish would be a record if it had not lost a lot of weight.

After thawing the fish, state Game and Fresh Water Fish Commission biologist Murray Stanford weighed it at 6 pounds, 15.75 ounces, which was heavy enough to eclipse Walker's mark set just a month before. Nelson's fish had lost 6.25 ounces due to freezing. It measured 21.75 inches in length and had a girth of 17 inches. If either fish would have been taken directly to a Commission biologist and certified scales, the mark could have been higher.

The next record, a 7.65 pound butterfly peacock, was set by Jesse Roberts of Miami on December 14, 1992 in the Hidden Lakes area of the Tamiami Canal (C-4) in Dade County. He was fishing from shore in this very productive West Kendall waterway using live shiners. The fish measured 22.3 inches long.

Giant Leap In Record Fish

Five days later, Philip Hines of Sunrise claimed the next record with a 8-pound, 12-ounce peacock caught in Black Creek (C-1) canal using a live shiner and 8-pound test line. He fought the butterfly peacock for about 15 minutes before landing it. Hines' 23-inch long fish with 18-inch girth was the seventh record in just over two years.

The 30 year old Hines was an avid largemouth bass fisherman before he accidentally caught a peacock while fishing for tarpon at the Miami International Airport lakes. Hines realized that pound-for-pound, peacocks are the hardest-fighting fish and soon focused almost all of his time on the species.

On March 11, 1993, Jerry Gomez of Miami landed a 9.08 pound peacock bass from Kendall Lakes in Dade County. The fish measured 22.4 inches long with a girth of 18.75 inches. The big fish had knocked off one of the trebles on Gomez's Rapala, who was using 6 pound test line and fishing from a 12 foot boat.

Maximum size of the butterfly peacock is poorly documented, but it is anticipated to be in the 11- or 12-pound range. Many potential new records exist in South Florida, according to Shafland. He recommends that anglers who think they have a record keep it alive until weighed by a Commission employee.

Speckled Peacock Growth

Speckled peacock, which must be released, get much larger. The first confirmed angler-reported catch of a speckled peacock weighed 11.37 pounds, was 26.25 inches long and had a girth of 19 inches. This fish was caught in the same area where it had been electro-fished by the Fish Commission 14 months earlier when it weighed 8.27 pounds and measured 24.5 inches. This catch proved the speckled peacock is biologically capable of living and growing in Southeast Florida canals. The Commission plans on increasing the stocking rate at a future date.

For current information on the peacocks of South Florida, check with one of the tackle shops that specialize in freshwater fishing. Several have a strong focus on the peacock bass and a "hotline" to daily activity and results in area canals and lakes.

Chapter 2

FLORIDA'S BUTTERFLY INTRODUCTIONS

The nation's newest, most explosive fishery

Florida's interest in peacock bass dates back to the early 1960's. Studies then documented excellent growth and successful reproduction in ponds, but the peacocks at that time seemed unable to overwinter, even in South Florida ponds. As a result, the studies were terminated.

Then, several years later, along came Paul L. Shafland of the Florida Game and Fresh Water Fish Commission. As Director of the Non-Native Fish Research Laboratory, Shafland wanted to experiment with peacocks again.

Today, peacock bass are geographically restricted in South Florida to the man-made canal systems since they cannot tolerate salt water or winter temperatures in shallower freshwater natural systems, according to the biologist. Shafland reviewed literature, personal communications, and water temperature records, and conducted an extensive assessment of Southeast Florida canal fish communities before proposing introduction of the fish. In 1984, he proposed introducing peacocks to the deep Dade County canals.

Shafland read previous reports of peacock bass introductions in Panama, Puerto Rico, Hawaii, Texas and Florida, and concluded that the introduction of peacock bass posed little, if any, adverse effects. Furthermore, he noted that their presence for even 2-3 years could create a sportfishery with significant socioeconomic and biological benefits. In Panama, Puerto Rico and Hawaii, introductions of peacock bass have been judged successes. Texas' and the earlier Florida pond attempts had been the only failures.

Distributional records of peacock bass from their native South America and introduced (Hawaii, Puerto Rico and Panama) ranges document their inhabiting only freshwater, even though in many areas they have access to marine waters.

During the past 20 years, fisheries biologists from Florida and Texas have conducted studies on peacock bass both in North and South America. All of these studies had a common objective of converting underutilized and overly abundant forage fishes in physically disturbed habitats to a top quality gamefish. No adverse impacts have been identified, however, the warm water nature of peacock bass severely limits their potential use.

Man's alteration of South Florida's natural water flow pattern caused by the construction of an extensive interconnecting canal system has created hospitable environments for establishment of many exotic fishes. Together with other native predators, largemouth bass have been unable to prevent rapid range extensions and population explosions of some introduced fishes which are of little value. Exotic fishes are so abundant in Dade County, Florida, according to Shafland, that they currently dominate the fish communities of major canal systems.

Annual Stocking of Butterfly Peacocks

Two peacock bass species were introduced into Southeast Florida canals to convert an overabundance of exotic forage fishes into desirable urban fisheries. Butterfly peacocks have over-wintered and reproduced every year since being introduced in 1984, and they are now considered a permanent component of these fish communities.

Actual stocking of the fish was initiated in October 1984, when 1,100 butterfly peacocks were released in approximately 10 canals from the Homestead area in Southern Dade north to around Pompano Beach. Over 90 percent of the fish were approximately two inches in length when stocked, but some were 14 inches. The butterfly peacocks are sexually mature in just one year and have since spawned naturally several times in the canals.

Speckled Introductions

Only 110 speckled peacocks were stocked into canals, the last of which were released in 1988. Speckled peacocks have been occasionally caught by fishermen. Although this species has successfully over-wintered at least two years, it is not yet considered to be established.

The butterfly peacocks are sexually mature in just one year.

    Shafland believes the maturation time for the speckled to be about 3 years and that the fish's minimum size at sexual maturity is about 10 pounds. That, coupled with the low number of speckled peacocks stocked and high fishing pressure exerted on these urban fisheries, should prevent a rapid creation of a trophy fishery. Furthermore, it is unlikely that a self-sustaining trophy fishery for this species could be established from a single stocking of even a much larger number of fish, according to Shafland.
    Nonetheless, according to Commission reports, the excellent survival, growth and possible reproduction of the small number of

speckled peacocks released in their studies suggests a trophy fishery could be created if it was stocked annually for at least 3-5 years.

"We introduced the speckled peacock because they grow larger," says Shafland. "We expect the butterfly peacock to be similar in size to the largemouth, as far as distributions. We have not collected a 10-pound largemouth from the canals in our electrofishing and sampling. We've gotten several over nine but never a true 10-pounder. We think the butterfly will be very similar in that respect."

"The peacocks are not expected to displace the current bass population," explains the biologist, "but rather supplement largemouth by helping them reduce the number of overly abundant forage."

Species Targeting

The butterfly peacock, though, is expected to be more successful numerically than the largemouth, according to the biologist. Therefore, if sport fishermen target the peacocks they should be able to catch more. There are ways to target each species, to some extent. For example, plastic worms won't attract peacock bass as they do largemouth.

Small live shiners will attract peacock bass more readily under most conditions. In fact, anglers using live bait will catch about eight peacocks for every one largemouth, according to Shafland. Tossing artificials in the canal systems will result in about one peacock bass caught for every one largemouth.

Peacocks in the canals are easy to catch on live bait, yet you can become more sophisticated and even use flies to catch them.

The Forage Base

In a study completed in the early 1980's, spotted tilapia averaged 25 percent by number and weight of all fishes throughout the Southeast Florida canal systems. In some of the canals, tilapia have literally taken over the waterway and comprise 50 percent of the fish population.

Biologists wanted to utilize that forage base and try to control the over-populated spotted tilapia. They knew that wouldn't be easy, since the small forage fish guard their young until they are about an inch long. Spotted tilapia are also substrate-spawning breeders and spawn every month of the year in the warm canal waters. They lay more eggs than other species of forage-size fish, like the blue tilapia. The spotted tilapia also grows to a smaller maximum size that blue tilapia and other potential forage species in the canal system.

The existence of butterfly peacocks has increased predator pressure on abundant but underutilized exotic forage fishes in the man-made, southeastern Florida canal system. As a result, a large portion of these less desirable exotics have been successfully converted into an important urban sportfishery.

Peacock bass have an insatiable appetite and will, however, forage on whatever fish is available. They'll even go after their smaller brothers, as the Commission biologists discovered on each additional stocking of the fish. When they go back to an area to supplement the crop with additional stockings, those from the previous introduction will move in and feed on the newly-introduced fingerlings.

Biscayne Aquifer Influence

The primary peacock bass study area was restricted to the coastal, man-made canal system of eastern (urban) Dade County. Peacock bass are incapable of tolerating water temperatures less than 60 degrees F, and the deep canals that were primarily constructed for drainage and flood control purposes seldom fall below 70 degrees. These canals are cut into the Biscayne Aquifer which is a shallow water table aquifer that offers spring influence.

Winter temperatures in natural Florida waters nearly always drop below 60 degrees F, except in ground water springs. In the eight years that Shafland has monitored water temperatures in the canal system, the coldest he's seen was 66 degrees. The warm waters are vital to the peacock bass over-wintering in the expansive waterway.

"The box-cut canals expose relatively small amounts of the waters to the weather," explains Shafland. "Probably just as important is the surficial aquifer, which allows underground water to flow from west to east. During the winter, storm water is stored in the East Everglades and that puts more head pressure, which causes a little underground flow into the canals."

If you swim in the canals, you can feel places where the warm water is coming in during the winter, according to the biologist. During cold fronts, some movement of the peacock bass is associated with water temperature. During a critical point when they begin to become stressed, they will seek out warmer water nearby.

The temperature limits their distribution in Florida, but it is also a safety factor, which prevents them from spreading to all waters around the state. The salinity tolerance limitations are similar to that of the largemouth bass. That gave the Commission assurance that the fish was safe and would be limited to the target area, the Southeast Florida canals only.

M ore than 10,000 butterfly pea-cocks and 2,600 large-mouth bass were caught during 1989 from a primary study canal which has a surface area of only 100 acres and length of 8 miles.

Exotic Population Problems

As head of the Boca Raton lab, Shafland has to view all exotic fish as potential problems. Several varieties commonly found in aquariums have been dumped by individuals into southeast Florida canals and have flourished. The infamous walking catfish, the pesky tilapia, the cute little Oscar and other exotics have gained a foothold in Florida's tropical climate. In fact, the state has 17 exotic species with permanent, "forever" populations.

Since a non-native fish species can change as it adapts to Florida waters and become competitive with existing species for food and habitat, Shafland has to be careful. He keeps a close watch over a variety of exotics in his 23-acre lab compound. Eight-foot high, barbed wire topped fences help contain his research subjects, but in the wild, a sudden population spurt may see them crowd out native fish, in some cases entirely.

The combination of the box-cut canal depths of more than 13 feet, widths generally less than 130 feet, typical shoreline wind breaks of buildings and trees, and inflow of groundwater from the aquifer provide one of the most receptive habitats imaginable in North America for many resident tropical fishes. That includes those that have been illegally introduced from Central and South America, Africa and Southeast Asia.

Black Creek Canal

The Black Creek Canal was chosen by the Game & Fresh Water Fish Commission as the initial study site because:

1. It had been extensively studied during past years.

2. Presence of flood and salinity control structures reduced the possibility of emigration from the area. Black Creek is located in east-central Dade County, and connects with Snapper Creek Canal to the north, the L-31N Canal to the west; and Biscayne Bay at Snapper Point and Cutler Ridge to the east.

The Black Creek Canal fish community is typical of Southeast Florida canal systems, made up of 23 species of which eight are exotic. Prior to the peacock's introduction, spotted tilapia, an African cichlid, dominated the fish community.

The main Black Creek Canal is about seven miles long, averages 10 feet wide and has vertical box-cut walls with depths of 13-17 feet. Shorelines are generally kept clear and periodically mowed, however, sizable sections have overhanging trees and brush. About 30 percent of the shoreline is residentially developed, the remainder being agricultural, road right-of-ways, commercial and a county sanitary landfill.

Several intermediate and small lateral canals off Black Creek Canal, as well as shallow roadside ditches, offer a variety of habitats available for fish. Utilization of man-made canals in their native range led Shafland to believe that the Black Creek Canal system would provide a suitable environment for peacock bass. It did, and the fish have expanded from there.

Miami's Urban Fishing Success

One creel study by the Commission showed that an acre of canal sustained 300 man-hours of fishing in a year, according to Shafland. By contrast, a well-regarded lake like Okeechobee receives only about three man-hours of fishing per acre in a year. This wide difference is due to two things: Miami has a large population near the canals, and it's also an ideal place for bank fishing; you generally need a boat to fish Okeechobee, and that eliminates a lot of fishing pressure.

According to a Annual Performance Reports by the Commission, the introduction of butterfly peacocks into Southeastern Florida urban canals has proven to be an overwhelming success in terms of its overall biological, sociological and economic impacts. The peacock bass is now the most sought after species by canal fishermen.

More than 10,000 butterfly peacocks and 2,600 largemouth bass were caught during 1989 from a primary study canal which has a surface area of only 100 acres and length of 8 miles. Fishing success for butterfly peacocks was excellent at 0.85 fish/hour, while largemouth bass were caught at a respectable 0.30 fish/hour. Monthly creel results from the primary peacock bass study canal show that the best months are January, with 1.58 caught per hour, and July, with 1.30. The best periods are the winter time months from November through February and the May through July warm weather months.

Fishing Hours and Places

These data confirm urban, man-made canals in Southeastern Florida can, and do, support good to excellent sportfishing opportunities. The results showed that more than two-thirds of the hours of canal fishing took place on weekends and holidays; and more fishermen fished during the four-hour mid-day creel time slot than before or after.

Other observations from fishermen interviews were (1) 76% fished from the bank versus 24% from boats; (2) 79% used rods and reels which require fishing licenses versus 21% who fished only with canepoles; (3) 58% used live bait versus 27% who used artificial lures and 15% who used other baits (e.g., bread dough or cut shrimp); (4) 52% of the live bait used was fish and 48% worms; and (5) 90% of the live fish used as bait were golden shiners.

From 1989 to 1992, redear sunfish averaged 42% more by weight and 306% more by number than during the previous three years. Redear sunfish has also been the most numerically abundant fish in the primary study canal during the last two years, something never before reported for a metropolitan Miami canal. Of the principal fishes, bluegill is the only native species that has decreased in terms of both total biomass and number during this time period, according to the studies.

Changes in the primary study canal fish community following the introduction of butterfly peacocks have been largely as anticipated, according to Shafland. These changes include a decrease in the targeted exotic prey species, spotted tilapia, an improvement in the forage-to-predator ratio, and establishment of an important urban fishery.

Southeast Florida Public Response

The following unsolicited testimonial to the G&FWF Commission from a young Dade County angler (age about 14), illustrates the importance of having quality fishing opportunities for youths in metropolitan areas:

"Dear Game and Fresh Water Fish Commission: I really enjoy fishing in Florida. My favorite gamefish is the newly stocked peacock bass. Some days I will spend eight to 10 hours trying to catch them. Even though I love to catch them, I feel I don't know enough about the species, such as breeding habits, feeding habits, their ability to withstand the cold and the reasons for stocking the beautiful fish in the south Florida canals. Enclosed is a picture of a peacock bass that I caught in June. I did keep this fish to be mounted, but I do practice catch and release on freshwater fish 99 percent of the time. Thank you for taking the time to read this letter and I hope to hear from you soon. Signed: John Peeler"

Southeast Florida urban canal sportfisheries were estimated to generate $19.6 - 39.2 million annually, with butterfly peacocks contributing an estimated $2.8 - 5.6 million. State sales taxes generated from these fisheries are estimated to be more than one million dollars annually. Thus, these renewable urban "natural" resources have a greater economic importance than previously recognized. A by-product is that the increased socioeconomic importance of canal fisheries reduces the tendency for area residents to discard trash into canals.

The organizer of half-day fishing trips for an eight-day IBM convention held in Miami reported more than $35,000 changed hands as a result of about 375 IBMers wanting to fish for butterfly peacocks. These fishermen landed 731 butterfly peacocks up to 5.19 pounds, 810 largemouth bass up to 7.75 pounds, 136 snook up to 8.13 pounds, and six tarpon up to 26 pounds. All these fish were taken from the urban lakes and canals immediately adjacent the Miami International Airport.

Organizers of the annual one-day Timberlake Kids Fishing Regatta reported more than 57 pounds of butterfly peacocks were caught from this 18 acre urban pond, mostly on live bait. Some kids caught as many as seven butterfly peacocks and largemouth bass combined from the bank; the largest butterfly peacock weighed in at 3.75 pounds while the biggest fish of the day was a 7.1-pound largemouth.

''One guy in particular, who's an avid largemouth bass fisherman, never could get his kids interested because they couldn't catch enough bass at any given time,'' says Shafland. ''Now, though, with a bucket of live bait, he can take his kids to the canals and get in on peacock bass action most any time.''

Chapter 3

THE WORLD'S BEST GIANT PEACOCK FISHERY

Venezuela's primitive and harsh Amazonas Territory

A band of friendly-looking natives on the shoreline were waving a towel at us as we motored by. A clearing atop the river bank just behind them revealed a dozen or more neatly-constructed, thatched-roof huts. The dozen or so men seemed to be wanting us to stop. I looked back at our guide to see if he had any inclination.

He put his flat hand shoulder-high and made a motion across his neck, as he kept on motoring down river. My partner and I knew what that gesture meant. It was not that we were the invited guests for dinner - it was that we WERE the dinner!

I am not sure whether our guide was exaggerating the potential danger or kidding us, but in the heart of the remote Amazonas Territory of Venezuela and Brazil, you learn to rely on the guide for such cautious advice.

On the bank, our ''friends''' glee seemed to turn to disappointment as our three-boat convoy motored right on by without stopping. After all, they were the legendary Yanomami Indians, supposedly the fiercest, most primitive tribe in the South American jungles. We weren't really very concerned for our safety. While the lore in several books about these particular Amazonas residents was probably outdated, there was no need for us to take any chances.

The lore I was there to check out was that the waters there were home to the world's most ferocious bass, the peacock, and that very

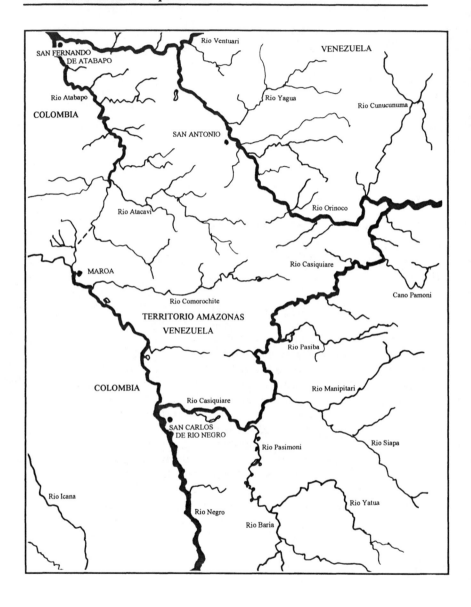

The waters of the South American jungle are home to the world's most ferocious bass, the peacock. Very probably a world record may exist there.

probably a world record may exist. Given my success on two different portions of the Amazon watershed during previous trips, I can attest to both. A world record from the Casiquiare River watershed, in particular, is not just a real possibility but a probability.

Monsters of the Casiquiare Watershed

In fact, on November 10, 1992, just a couple of weeks prior to my visit, Bert Bookout caught a 25-pound, 8-ounce peacock from those waters on a fly rod. That's just one pound off the all-tackle world mark! Bookout's fish was 39 1/2 inches long and had a 24 inch girth. It was the largest caught during the 1992/93 season; last season's big "official" fish from this watershed, a 24 pounder, was caught by woman angler Ami Nash of Birmingham. It was certified by IGFA as a 20-pound line class world record.

Another peacock from these waters last year was not weighed on certified scales (all they had along was a small, inaccurate 20-pound scale), but it measured 41 inches in length and 25 inches in girth! Check out the Weight Computer in Chapter 15 to see just how big this fish possibly was.

Some destinations offer up an occasional giant, but these waters yield numerous peacock bass over 20 pounds - and correspondingly, within reach of the 26 pound, 8 ounce all-tackle record. In fact,

*A*ndy Rockwell of Dallas, TX, shows off his 15-1/2 pound Amazonas peacock.

according to Alechiven Tour's U.S. agent Dick Ballard, only a few people to visit the Casiquiare tributary lagoons have ever fished a week without landing a 20 pound peacock. Over 60 anglers have hit that mark, and I, happily, was one of them.

The Guayana Highlands' Tepuis and Lagoons

Our small group of five anglers (Andy Rockwell of Dallas, Pete Vermeulen of San Diego, Dick Ballard of Springfield, MO, Joe Kubisz of Key Largo and myself) caught and released 38 peacocks over 12 pounds during the week. The largest, caught by Vermeulen, weighed 22 pounds. Only two in our group didn't catch a 20-pounder, and one angler had been there before and had caught four that big. He tallied seven between 18 1/2 and 19 3/4 pounds, so don't feel sorry for him. A tally of the lures those 38 big peacocks hit was as follows: 15 on Woodchoppers, 5 on Redfins, 4 on small Jerkin' Sams, 1 on a Bill Lewis Super Trap, 1 on a small topwater plug.

The location of this giant peacock bass fishery is the Casiquiare River watershed located at the extreme southern tip of Venezuela near the borders of Brazil and Colombia. The Casiquiare joins the Rio Negro on the eastern border of Colombia and the Rio Orinoco

There were few creature comforts at the campsite they called "Alechita."
A 50-foot long native "bongo" (dugout canoe) served as the supply
boat for the campsite and as quarters for the Indian guides and crew.

north and east of the town of San Carlos de Rio Negro. The Casiquiare actually connects Venezuela's huge Orinoco River to Brazil's massive Amazon River by way of the Rio Negro.

Most of our fishing took place in the lagoons off one of the Casiquiare tributaries, the Pasimoni River. After taking commercial jets to Caracas and onto Puerto Ayacucho, we boarded a small single-engine prop job and flew past mile-high flattop rocky hills called "Tepuis." The flight over mountain remnants and Tepuis stretching above the Guayana Highlands north of the Rio Negro lasted two hours. We landed on a dirt strip carved into the jungle at the remote village of San Carlos. After a three-hour boat ride from there along the Casiquiare and into the Pasimoni, we arrived at our remote campsite.

Alechita Creature Comforts

There were few creature comforts at the campsite they called "Alechita." We basically camped out under a "Churuata" or thatched-roof shelter. They did have a pair of propane-fired refrigerators and stove, tables and chairs in a separate dining shelter.

The Pasimoni River has scattered boulders throughout its 50 miles, but not much else in the way of emergent structure.

We drank bottled water and soft drinks, and had simple but delicious meals. Personal hygiene was comforted by an outhouse at the campsite and by bathing in the river. A shower fashioned from a 400-gallon drum of river water on a tripod was inaccessible due to high water the week we were there.

We took our chances regarding the fearsome ''candiru'', an inch-long parasite that enters the orifices of the human body and lodges itself by spines. The fish is invisible until filled with blood and has to be removed surgically. The fish is said to be attracted to urine in the water. That could be just ''camp talk,'' but we definitely were careful when taking a dip in the river.

We slept under mosquito netting on cots and hammocks, although the bugs were not bad. A good insect lotion was employed at dawn and dusk to keep ''no see-ums'' away, and long-sleeved shirts and long pants were generally worn for protection from afternoon sun and the biting bugs after dark. A 50-foot long native ''bongo'' (dugout canoe) with 55-hp motor served as the supply boat for the campsite and as quarters for the Indian guides and crew.

We fished from 16-foot aluminum V-hull boats with large, long-handled nets, padded swivel-seats and 45-hp outboard motors. The Alechiven guides were mostly Indians (not the Yanomami) from the

During normal water conditions, the Pasimoni offers some giant peacocks.

The Pasiba River Passage

The Pasiba River, a tributary of the Casiquiare, offers several good lagoons with difficult access. At the lower end of the river, there is a large lagoon which is fairly productive, but better fishing can be had above it. When water levels are normal in the Pasiba, there are numerous sandbars to pull the boat over to get to the best fishing.

When the lagoons are fairly dry, the fish move out into the river itself in deep pools. You'll find them in an area where the current is relatively slack and where a deep pool exists. The pools are normally lined with big boulders, but the big fish are in the middle of those pools. Around the shoreline rocks, there are plenty of little peacocks to catch, and there are piranha anywhere there is current in the river.

"If you cast to a round rock, you might catch a small butterfly peacock or a piranha," says avid Pasiba River visitor T.O. McLean. "But, the big peacocks are not in the same areas as the smaller fish. When fishing in the Pasiba River, you have to fish the deep holes in the middle to catch the very big peacocks."

The author was awarded four line class word records by the National Fresh Water Fishing Hall of Fame in Hayward, WI. They included a 19-pounder (left) and a 20-pound peacock (right). The latter was taken on 10-lb Trilene XT monofilament line.

"That's where I had on my largest peacock ever," claims McLean. "I made a cast over toward some rocks and hooked a butterfly peacock that weighed maybe four pounds. I was bringing him in, when I saw a shadow behind the fish. A huge peacock then swallowed the butterfly, the fish and my five-inch long Jerkin' Sam topwater lure."

"I set the hook and played the huge fish for a little while, but I never really got a hook into it," McLean continues. "My partner and I both agreed that this fish was well up in the twenties and possibly world record size. Finally, the fish just spat out the little peacock and went on his way."

McLean has seen payara, the saber-toothed menace, come up and swallow a small peacock on a few different occasions. One of 15 to 20 pounds would grab a four- or five-pound peacock. On two different occasions, he observed those payara being netted - not because they were hooked, but because they wouldn't let go of the peacock.

The fishing is normally best on the Venezuelan waters off the Casiquiare from December through the second week of April. As you can imagine, bookings for this Amazonas jungle trip are heavy, but Ballard (Fishing Adventures, 140 E. Ritter, Republic, MO 65738; phone 800-336-9735) can provide additional information and Viasa and American flight schedules for those interested.

I am sure that several world record peacock bass exist in these areas. Yanomami Indians or not, I will be going back after one. Sleeping on a cot and bathing in the river is worth the numerous topwater explosions from fierce 15 to 25 pound bass!

Line Class World Records

I traveled to the Casiquiare watershed with some light line aimed at setting some line class world records with the National Fresh Water Fishing Hall of Fame record-keeping agency. Four of my catches have been recognized as such. While I've personally caught and released about seven peacocks over 15 pounds in a half dozen trips prior to this one, I quickly caught my largest ever on the first morning, a 19-pounder.

That personal best didn't last long, as I was fortunate to catch, weigh, measure and release a 20 pounder. Add to that giant another seven or eight over 15 pounds during four days of fishing this area, and you have exciting record-chasing.

How can you receive four world records simultaneously? You prepare to get them. The records for the four peacock bass, which weighed up to 20 pounds, were established in the 14, 16, 20 and unlimited pound line classes. The heaviest fish, a 20-pound peacock, was taken on 10-pound Trilene XT monofilament line. The strength of the line qualified the record fish in the 14 pound line class. The giant peacock measured 36 inches long and had a 22-inch girth.

Three of the fish were caught on a giant Woodchopper topwater bait, while a fourth record fish fell to a Super Trap vibrating plug. I had various weights of Trilene line spooled on Daiwa Procaster baitcasting reels seated on Berkley Series One rods. For more information on the line class records, write Larsen's Outdoor Publishing, 2640 Elizabeth Place, Lakeland, FL 33813.

Chapter 4

VENEZUELA'S MASSIVE LAKE GURI

Check out the remote reaches of this giant impoundment

One of the most exciting fresh water destinations in the world may be Lake Guri, formed by the construction of the Raul Leoni Dam, the world's second largest hydro-electric facility. The lake was formed over a ten-year period during the damming of the Caroni River, near its confluence with the Orinoco River. The dam now supplies 75 percent of the entire country's electrical power.

Lake Guri is the second largest man-made lake in the world, stretching 80 miles long and averaging 22 miles wide. It is reported to be up to 640 feet deep. Lake Guri forms 2,000 square miles of flooded forests in rolling hills in the southeastern state of Bolivar, about 325 miles from the capital of Caracas. Part of the lake, because it covers the valleys between the hills, is more like a series of twisting channels. From the air, it is the most beautiful lake that I have seen.

The habitat here is tremendous. Mammoth trees over 100 feet high stand upright under the surface, and their tops are where peacocks often congregate. Along the shoreline of the coves and islands are rocks, some vegetation and more brush. There are floating ''gardens'' which are floating bogs, logs and placid pools that offer exciting fishing opportunities.

Fish can be at any depth; there's no thermocline to restrict them. On one trip, we took a temperature reading and found just 4 degrees difference between the surface and 85 feet down. Both peacocks and

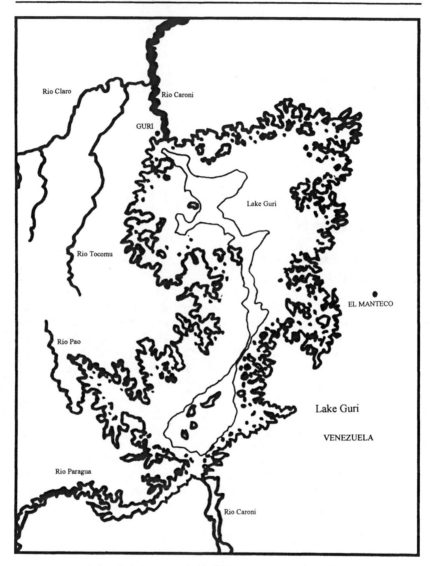

payara prowl the deepest trunks of the biggest trees. The biggest trees remaining in the reservoir are not very brushy on top, so they offer deep jigging opportunities while holding the boat beside them.

Guri contains both the speckled peacock and the butterfly peacock, with the latter comprising only about five percent of the population

T he habitat on Lake Guri is tremendous. The tops of mammoth trees are just under the water's surface, where peacocks often congregate. Along the shoreline of the coves are rocks, vegetation and brush. Floating "gardens" of bogs, logs and placid pools offer exciting fishing opportunities.

of "pavon," as they are commonly referred to here. The lake had no resident population of peacocks, according to Venezuelan sources, and it was stocked during its fill operation in the mid-80's. Some local ranchers reportedly had stocked their ponds with peacocks from the Orinoco River, so some larger "brood stock" fish were probably present as the ponds were inundated during the fill.

While piranha was the predominant species in the lake initially, as the peacocks grew, the former became excellent forage. Today, you seldom catch a piranha on large artificial lures (using bait is another matter), and peacocks up to 20 pounds swim in these waters. When water was first backed up behind the dam, anglers averaged more than 30 peacocks a day. When the dam was closed in 1986, the fish spread out as the lake doubled. The average catch decreased.

In my 20 to 25 days of fishing the lake over a three year period, I can say I averaged about 12 peacocks each day. On good days that number was double and on my last two days of my very last trip to the lake, I caught only about seven or eight fish. For the non-experienced peacock angler, those rates would be considered very high. On many of my better days, others in the group had trouble locating and catching more than a few peacocks.

L *ake Guri peacocks over 13 pounds are fairly rare. The author's largest on this body of water was a 16-pounder.*

Catch-and-Release Restrictions

Fortunately, visiting anglers are limited to catch-and-release fishing (with an occasional exception made for shore-lunch or an evening meal). Numerous peacocks of 9 to 12 pounds do exist in the lake, and most good fishermen fishing the right lures will catch one or two every day or so. Peacocks over 13 are fairly rare on the lake. My largest of 16 pounds provided an experience I won't forget.

The lake has been described as "one of the fishiest-looking places you could ever go." It is, and the peacock bass are abundant and eager to pounce on most any kind of lure, if you can locate them.

In my four trips to Lake Guri, I fished those fertile waters extensively. On my first visit I stayed at Hato Puedpa (Puedpa Ranch) near the village of El Manteco. A transfer agent met us at the Maiquetia International Airport just outside Caracas. After overnighting in Caracas, our six-angler contingent flew on a small airline to the beautiful mining town of Puerto Ordaz, a community of 130,000. We were then driven via Land Rovers on a scenic two-hour drive through the countryside to the ranch.

Hato Puedpa was the country retreat of former President Raul Leoni, now deceased, for whom the dam was named. The property

Except for the occasional shore lunch or evening meal, visiting anglers are limited to catch-and-release fishing.

has been in the Moreno family for over 100 years and is currently owned by his son in law, Gonzalo Moreno Leoni.

We readied our gear on the scenic, wide verandah. Lounging in the hammocks that beckoned guests for an afternoon nap had to wait. We had fish to catch, and couldn't wait to hit the water that afternoon.

Coves, Bogs and Flooded Timber

The upper half of Guri Reservoir is a maze of thousands of islands, bogs, arms, coves, bays and flooded timber everywhere. As a result, establishing a productive pattern is vital to success. Schools of large peacock bass will do battle with almost anything coming into their territory, if you can locate that territory. If not, the catch may be slim.

The island shorelines in Guri vary from rocks to sand to mud, with a perimeter barrier of inundated forests. Knowing the bottom composition can pay big dividends. The entire bottom was left undisturbed before the flooding, creating excellent habitat for the fishery, most of it rock or sand. The better soil, however, according to my experience, is mud. The tannic stained waters are full of visible cover, but you can't see the bottom below.

The fishing here is some of the most exciting I've ever experienced. The aggressive pavon are not only schooling fish but are extremely

The upper half of Guri Reservoir is a maze of thousands of islands, bogs, arms, coves, bays and flooded timber everywhere.

competitive. In the right areas, such as mud-bottomed points and road beds, doubles are common. Time after time, my wife Lilliam and I hooked a second fish swimming beside a hooked pavon. The fish averaged four to five pounds and took to the air several times when hooked. They exploded at the surface and tore up lures that American manufacturers never designed for these fish.

Island Saddles and Points

The best spot that I identified was a mud "saddle" between two islands. The water was about 15 feet and shallowed up to about two. From depths of 8 to 12 feet we caught and released 25 acrobatic pavon each day. The spot was different from the nearby island points that had rocky compositions. It also had many more fish.

Several of our fish were in the six- to seven-pound class with a few weighing up to 12 pounds. I lost one at the boat estimated at 20 pounds. My 20 pound test TriMax held and the reel's drag was effective, but my lure was not designed for a giant pavon. The fish leaped five times during the five minute battle and was a foot from the waiting net when the hooks pulled free. Upon examination, I discovered that my three treble hooks were straightened out.

The Sinister and Ugly

Several anglers in our group fished beside giant, flooded oak trees near submerged river channels and fought some huge Dracula-

The fishing here an exciting experience due to the aggressive pavon being extremely competitive.

like payara between 14 and 22 pounds. They had a ball by vertically jigging spoons at the right depth and then tussling with the leapers at boat-side when they surfaced. The schools of silvery, fanged fish seemed to hang out together in depths of 30 to 70 feet and were easily denoted on the electronics.

When fishing for the saber-toothed payara, wire leaders are recommended. These are the most unusual trophy you may see. Two long fangs fit into slots in the upper mouth and the tips protrude through the top of the fish's head. They have a bright bluish backbone. When hooked, the payara rips off line as it twists and leaps in an attempt to throw the lure. They grow to about 30 pounds in some waters, so they are a formidable opponent at any weight.

While pavon and payara get most of the attention on Guri, there are 11 other fish species that can also be caught by traveling anglers. These include the caribe, a relative of the ferocious piranha, the curbinata, and the popular catfish. All are delicious to eat. The prehistoric guavina, with werewolf appearance, and the toothy amara that resembles a black mudfish of U.S. waters, are other fish to be caught. The latter makes rocket-like leaps if pressure is applied during the runs. Both grow to 20 pounds or so in the lake and strike artificials.

The guides, while knowing the lake from the navigation standpoint, had little knowledge of depths. The boats did not have electric trolling motors, or even paddles, which should tell you the sophistication of the craft.

A nglers can fish next *to giant, flooded trees near submerged river channels and find some huge Dracula-like payara between 14 and 22 pounds.*

Guri Lodge - The Oasis

Just 45 minutes on wide, paved highways from Puerto Ordaz is the relatively new fishing operation called Guri Lodge. I've been to the lodge three times and enjoyed the hospitality and fishing each time. The lodge was built in the early 60's by the Venezuelan government to house engineers and VIP's who were working on the dam while under construction.

The accommodations, food, boats and motors, guides and management at the three-story Guri Lodge are as good as I have found in South America. They now have eight Ranger Bass Boats parked at the marina just down the hill from the lodge. The hilltop resort is part of a complex which includes a supermarket, bar, restaurant, cinema, bowling alley and gift shop. The lodge, with a pool you won't have time to use, is run by a super-nice young couple, Jacob and Andi Elias. They can accommodate up to 16 anglers per week and do everything in their power to make the trip a success.

Timing The Bite

Guri Reservoir in Venezuela has been one of my favorite fishing destinations for several years. For the first couple of years, it didn't seem to make much difference when you fished Guri Lake. Big peacocks seemed to be found all over the lake any month of the year. Now a pattern has been established at Guri. During the months of April to October, fishing can vary!

I believe that the inconsistent fishing is due to the fluctuation of lake water levels throughout the summer months. During the "cooler", drier months of October through March, Guri produces the most consistently good fishing. Water levels are much more stable at this time. Air temperatures in this part of Venezuela are fairly consistent throughout the year.

January through March are the most popular months, and this period usually books full each year. October through December are just as good, as stated above, and the fishing "pressure" is lighter then. In actuality, there will only be about 12 to 15 boats per day on the 2,000 square miles of reservoir in the "busy" season.

Most peacocks spawn on Guri in April, but many have multi spawns and do so deeper in the lake than elsewhere. On the Orinoco River, for example, the peacocks normally spawn shallower and do so in February.

Peacocks sometimes school in open water on the big lake. They can be seen in the early morning and then again late in the day churning up the water chasing small baby piranha or other baitfish that the guides on Guri call "sardines." During high sun hours, they mostly ambush unlucky prey.

America's Cup Fishing Tournament

Competitive fishing can be fun, particularly when the real quarry are peacock bass. Add the fellowship between the six-man American team and the six-man Venezuelan team in a setting like Lake Guri and hospitality provided by tournament headquarters, Guri Lodge, and you have the makings for a great event.

Two America's Cup Fishing Tournaments were held on Venezuela's Lake Guri, and I attended the second one. An American team composed of several U.S. television outdoor show hosts battled a contingent of dignitary anglers from Venezuela. The friendly

A six-man American team and a six-man Venezuelan team participated in a friendly peacock bass fishing competition on Lake Guri.

competition also attracted several sponsors and outdoor writers from the States. The peacock bass cooperated fully, and all anglers found them aggressive. Several contestants caught a tournament-imposed, three-fish daily limit weighing over 30 pounds; that's a very respectable 10-pound average size fish.

The average size of peacock in the waters around Guri Lodge is around 5 or 6 pounds, but several between 9 and 12 pounds were taken by the contestants and media. Several monsters were caught, including the tournament's biggest fish caught by Cesar Toledo of the American team, which weighed 17.06 pounds. Renee Garcia of EDELCA caught the largest peacock for the Venezuelan team, a 15-pounder.

The winner of the tournament was well known outdoor TV personality and professional fisherman Roland Martin, who caught 87.02 pounds over the three day event. Each of the six American contestants was paired with a Venezuelan angler each of the three days. They fished from the 20-foot-long Ranger bass boats powered by 200 horsepower Yamaha outboards. The well-equipped rigs, manned by local guides, were necessary, but allowed the anglers to cover only a small portion of the huge Lake Guri.

The Competition Connection

The major fishing event started taking shape well before the contestants climbed into their boats. Outdoor travel tour operators, Dick Ballard, of Fishing Adventures in Springfield, Missouri and Jimmy Houston, of Jimmy Houston Travel in Tulsa, Oklahoma worked with Jacobo Elias of Guri Lodge, VIASA Airways and the Venezuelan government to establish tournament logistics.

While the contestants had their only practice round, the media and industry sponsors got serious. From the average depths of 6 to 12 feet, the press (and later the contestants) caught and released 15 to 25 acrobatic peacock bass each day. Several of the media and sponsor's fish were in the 11 pound class, and a few were even larger. I hooked and landed one that weighed 16 pounds, and Berkley Bedell of Berkley Co. caught a fat 14 pounder.

The tournament anglers were limited to 14-pound test line, and several lost big fish until they added long heavy-duty leaders and stronger hooks to their plugs. The Venezuelan team caught 177.88 pounds, while the American team compiled 390.58 pounds in the three days of the 1990 American's Cup.

The Guri Lodge guides were quite knowledgeable about the lake from the navigation standpoint, as well as where the peacock bass could be located. The comfortable boats had electric trolling motors, depth sounders and live wells to keep the fish alive for the weigh-ins held each afternoon at the Guri Lodge Marina. Afterwards, the bass were returned to the lake to swim off.

Guri's Golden History

Fishing with light tackle did not receive much attention in the area until the late 70's. The damming of the reservoir provided an angling site for various petroleum company executives from overseas who were headquartered in Puerto Ordaz. Soon, these anglers realized that their lures were attracting the pavon and other fish. Word slowly spread over the years, and eventually resulted in a promotional opportunity for the region.

The Guri experience is memorable. Truly at the end of the road, this is where civilization meets wilderness. Caiman (small crocodile), parrots, monkeys, jaguars and tapirs are in and around the shorelines of the lake. There are just a few commercial fishermen working these waters, and the remainder of the handful of boats one may see are miners on their way to one of the many precious stone mines in the area. Gold prospectors search the shallows and diggings just off the

T he Guri experience was memorable for the author's wife, Lilliam. On her first trip, these waters yielded her largest fish - a 13-pounder.

lake for nuggets. From the lake, this impoundment has similarities to Corps of Engineers projects.

The climate in that part of the country is perfect for the shore lunches each noon, and the scenery is spectacular. I have enjoyed delicious pavon stuffed with tomatoes, green peppers and onion, wrapped in aluminum foil and then grilled, and pavon and curbinata cut in filets and fried. Perhaps the most unique menu was fried caribe (piranha) which, as it turned out, was a delicious sweet meat.

Most tour operators will arrange side trips to natural wonders in this part of the country. One of the most popular is a day's trip to little-known Angel Falls. This excursion will reveal a totally new world. Angel Falls are the highest waterfalls in the world, toppling 1,212 feet from the top of a jungle-covered cliff. Visitors can arrange a morning flight to the falls and enjoy lunch at the Camp Canaima at the base of the mountains.

Chapter 5

THE ORINOCO TRIBUTARIES OF VENEZUELA

Great peacock fishing in the jungles

Venezuela is called the "Paradise of Pavons" because of the fish's development, size and range. There are several excellent peacock fisheries in the country. Some, such as the Ventuari, Capanaparo and Cinaruco rivers, are tributaries to the Orinoco River. Others, like the Pasimoni and Pasiba, are tributaries to the Casiquiare and are discussed in Chapter 3.

Venezuelan biologists usually describe three species of peacock: the speckled or grande pavon *(Cichla Temensis)*, the butterfly pavon *(Cichla Orinocensis* or *Ocellaris)* and the royal pavon (*Cichla nigrolineatus* or *intermedia*). Not all are native to all waters. Stocking of *C. ocellaris* first occurred in 1953 in the Guarataro Reservoir. Pavon were introduced in many waters since a 1964 stocking into the Rio Caroni prior to Lake Guri's impoundment.

Speckled and butterfly were introduced in the Reservoirs Majaguas in Portuguesa, Guanapito and Tamanaco in Guarico, Aragua de Barcelona in Anzoategui, Burro Negro in Lago Maracaibo, El Ysiro in Falcon, Camatagua in Aragua, Lagartijo in Miranda, Cuenca del Tuy, Cumaripa in Yaracuy, El Cigarron and El Pueblito in Guarico, Cuenca del Caribe, El Pao-La Balsa in Cojedes, Guataparo in Carabobo, and many other impoundments.

Speckled and butterfly pavon are found throughout the country, except in the Cuyuni and Guarapiche rivers, where only the latter is found. The royal peacock inhabits only the regions from the Rio Cinaruco southward.

The butterfly has been introduced in numerous Venezuelan reservoirs and other waters that never had peacocks before.

The running and clear waters of the Orinoco and its creeks constitute a natural habitat for the peacock's life and reproduction. The geographic exception is the triangle formed by Rio Apure, Rio Portuguesa and Rio Guarico whose waters are too clayish. The main channel of the Orinoco offers turbid waters that are likewise not conducive to the peacock. The peacock must be able to see its prey in the water.

Caracas' Nearby Pavon Spots

In the large state of Guarico, just south of Caracas, the Rio Guariquito offers excellent fishing. Despite years of commercial fishing and sport fishing pressure, it is still one of the best rivers in Venezuela. The closest pavon fishery to Caracas and one of the best in the country is Camatagua Reservoir, the principal water supply to the nation's capital city.

The Ernesto Leon Dam, built across the Rio Guarico in 1968, created the national reserve called Camatagua Reservoir. Its watershed near the mountains receives almost daily rains, but seldom does it rain over the lake. Peacocks were introduced to the 6-mile-long lake in 1972, and today, a few fish up to 22 pounds swim in these waters.

To reach the impoundment, which is about 60 miles south of the capital, take the highway from Caracas to Valencia and exit toward Charallave. Travel to the road San Casimiro-Camatagua where a sign will direct you to the recreational tourist camp on Camatagua. A fee is charged to enter, and there are rental boats, cabins and picnicking available. There are three dirt and one concrete ramps available. No fishing permit is necessary. Unfortunately, there are no creel limits here.

The shores of the reservoir are covered with vegetation. Peacocks bite here year around, but 9 a.m. to 3 p.m. are best for fishing artificials. The quiet coves not exposed to the wind are best. The peacocks hang out in water three to seven feet deep outside of the algae beds. Topwater baits are not as effective on this reservoir as they are on other Venezuelan waters. Slow trolling near the vegetation with spoons, spinnerbaits, vibrating baits and minnow plugs can be effective. On a good day, three fishermen in a boat may catch 10 to 15 peacocks of up to 5 pounds; peacocks over 10 pounds are not frequently caught here.

Central and Southern Venezuela

Let's look at some of the Orinoco tributaries that have substantial populations of peacock bass. In the state of Monagas in central eastern Venezuela, North American oilmen discovered the peacock and began to fish them in the numerous lagoons and rivers. The better waters included Laguna Grande near Maturin, Laguna de San Antonio, Laguna San Pablo, Rio Morichal Largo, Palital, and Mamo.

The Rio Guarapiche and Rio Cuyuni also offer good fishing for butterfly peacock. The abundant pavon are native due to the rivers' connection with the Orinoco delta watershed, but they are small compared to those in other states. Rarely are they over five pounds, but the fishing is interesting due to the natural beauty of the lagoons. The growing fishing pressure in this region is thankfully mitigated by the rainy season which makes those fishing areas inaccessible.

Bolivar, Apure and Guarico have much larger peacocks and are the best states in the central part of the country. Some of the best known rivers in Guarico are Aguaro, San Bartolo, Mocapra, San Jose and Guanarito. In the Amazonas territories, peacocks are found in Las Carmelitas, and the Pamoni and Pacivia Rivers.

Other pavon fishing has occurred in Rio Sipao, Rio Tucurigua, Rio Aro and the large Rio Caura in the north central part of Bolivar. Other regional rivers include Aricagua, Carana, Tirita, Corrientoso and Suapo. Accessibility to those areas are limited to the summer and is reportedly difficult.

According to Venezuelan biologists, illegal commercial fishing of peacocks is the worst enemy of the sport fishery in that country.

"The construction of new roads to many of these areas has facilitated access to many of the above areas," one told me. "That has resulted in more commercial pressure and illegal sales of pavon. The sale is prohibited, but the lack of willingness on the part of the authorities to enforce this law has become the worst enemy of sport fishing and could even preclude the extermination of the species."

Brown Rock Gardens

The Ventuari River (which is part of the headwaters of the Orinoco River) has produced great fishing for anglers over the past half dozen years. It lies south of the Capanaparo and Cinaruco rivers in the Amazonas Territory, the southern leg of the country bordered by Colombia to the west and Brazil to the south and east. The unexplored jungles and highlands surrounding the waterway of rivers, streams, and swamps is a unique setting for angling activities.

The Ventuari River (which is part of the headwaters of the Orinoco River) has produced great fishing for anglers over the past half dozen years.

Fishing for Ventuari peacocks generally takes place in the abundant backwater lagoons and slackwater sloughs off the main channel. For numbers of peacock with little interruption from other species, the fertile lagoons are the place to be. Schools of peacocks roam the shallows and mid-depth open water seeking any forage.

The lagoon and river banks are lined with savanna grass and a labyrinth of vines. The Ventuari waterway spans from 100 yards up to a half mile at its widest point, dotted with brown rocks. There is good fishing around the rock islands or ''gardens'' for a variety of species. Peacocks are normally found around current breaks on the downstream sides of the rocky islands. Casts to the bolder crevices and cracks will often result in a peacock explosion.

Most of the peacocks over 20 pounds have been taken around the rock gardens, according to local guides. River fishing, however, is primarily productive for piranha, payara, sardinata and the smaller butterfly peacocks. In all, there are a dozen or so exotic species to be caught in these waters including some giant 100 pound-plus catfish.

Ventuari Lagoons

Ventuari lagoons normally offer very good fishing in the 5-foot deep flats and along shorelines. They reportedly yield better numbers

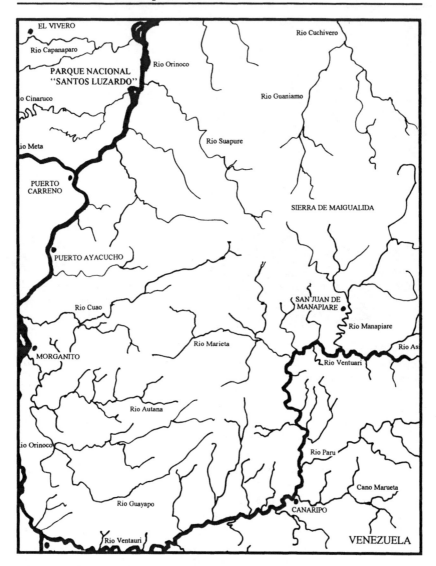

EL VIVERO

Rio Cuchivero

Rio Capanaparo

Rio Orinoco

PARQUE NACIONAL
"SANTOS LUZARDO"

Rio Guaniamo

o Cinaruco

io Meta

Rio Suapure

PUERTO
CARRENO

SIERRA DE MAIGUALIDA

PUERTO AYACUCHO

SAN JUAN DE
MANAPIARE

Rio Cuao

Rio Manapiare

Rio As

Rio Marieta

MORGANITO

Rio Ventuari

Rio Autana

io Orinoco

Rio Paru

Cano Marueta

Rio Guayapo

CANARIPO

Rio Ventauri

VENEZUELA

of peacock bass than currently does Lake Guri. On the average,
though, Guri's peacocks are a little bigger. Often, the very best
fishing is in almost "virgin" lagoons a few hours boat ride from the
nearest encampment. Fishing pressure on the lagoons seems to have
a negative effect. Fishing those that have been given a rest is wise.

D uring the dry season on the Ventuari lagoons, peacocks exhaust the food supply and get very hungry. They remain aggressive until the rains return.

If you have to make casts for 15 or 20 minutes to generate a strike, it may be time to move to another spot. If action slows, then move around the bend or to another lagoon.

During the rainy season (June through October), water levels rise and peacocks move into the heavy cover of shallow lagoons and sloughs. When water levels decrease after a few months, many peacocks are stranded in the deep backwater pools. During the dry (December through April), they pretty much exhaust the food supply. The peacocks get hungry, very hungry! They remain there in an aggressive posture until the rains return, and the cycle is repeated.

To access the Ventuari, you'll fly to Puerto Ayacucho. From there, a small plane ride leaves all traces of civilization behind. You'll fly through valleys between peaks and "tepuis" (flat-topped mountains), past waterfalls to a dirt roadway landing strip.

In these waters, you're sure to see 25-foot-long "bongos" which are made from single tree trunks. You may also see freshwater stingrays and eels, otters and bottlenose dolphin in the lagoons and river areas. On the banks may be Baniba and Piaroa Indian villages and colorful bird or animal life.

At the confluence of the Ventuari and Orinoco Rivers is the popular Manaka Lodge. First opened in 1987, it has booked full each week from December through mid-April, with the maximum capacity of only 8 to 10 anglers per week. Texan T. O. McLean has visited the Manaka Lodge 17 times and believes that the destination offers some of the best facilities of any of the camps in that region of Venezuela.

Cinaruco River

In the barren llanos (plains) south of San Fernando de Apure lies an emerald ribbon of water called the Cinaruco (sometimes spelled Sinaruco) River. It's about 275 miles southwest of Caracas. The better fishing here is often in the lagoons off the main river channel. Dense jungle parallels the river. Few residents live along the waterways, but you might see jaguars, tapirs, capybaras or monkeys.

The rich, green waters upstream from the Cinaruco's mouth are home to lots of peacock bass. They hang out in the narrow guts behind sandbars where careful waders can easily access them. When wading, be ever mindful of the South American freshwater stingray. Like other creatures that evolve along the equator, it is a little bigger than life, a little tougher and a little meaner.

Peacocks feed in big concentrations along the river banks and lagoons in this area. The Cinaruco reportedly offers anglers a chance at catching 30 to 60 fish a day, some weighing up to 12 pounds. This area of the Venezuela outback is potentially problematic, though, due to nearby Colombia drug activities. Some of the drug bandidos seem to have an appetite for snatching small planes from isolated dirt strips in that particular region, according to local sources.

The best fishing on the 200 mile-long Cinaruco River is from mid-November through March during the drier months. Roads allow access to the area now, according to a Venezuelan source. Fish in many places along the river are often bigger than 5 pounds, but are seldom larger than 12 pounds; a 15 pounder would demand everyone's attention. There are plenty of payara here, as an option. In the state of Apure, the Cano La Pica, Rio Claro, Rio Cunacuro, and Rio Cunavichito also produce pavon over 12 pounds.

Chapter 6

BRAZIL'S AMAZON BASS

Gangs of tucunare roam the tributary lagoons

The peacock bass action on the lagoons off the Trombetas, Madeira and Cumina Rivers in Brazil can be red hot in the fall. The tributaries to the renown Amazon River offer a unique fishery in the heart of the world's largest rain forest. There's enough bites each day from peacock bass and other species such as piranha (which may average four pounds each), suribim and the saber-toothed payara to keep things very interesting.

Numerous peacocks between 12 and 18 pounds promise topwater action an angler won't soon forget. It is very possible on the Trombetas watershed for two anglers tossing or trolling large surface plugs to catch and release 35 peacocks weighing 350 pounds in one day! Other areas west of Manaus hold the same promise (see next chapter). South of Manaus is the fabulous Madeira watershed, which currently may be Brazil's best peacock fishery.

I recently accompanied Dick Ballard of Fishing Adventures, to the Brazilian Rain Forests to check out some of several peacock bass opportunities that the tour operator offers in Brazil. One was based out of Port Trombetas on the Trombetas River, a tributary of the Amazon which drains 2,722,000 square miles (an area almost the size of the United States).

Dick and I arrived to check out the numerous lakes and lagoons in the area on a seven-day Package trip (five full days of fishing, plus a half-day of fishing upon arrival and a half day prior to departure). This was the only full season for the operation in the Port Trombetas

The Trombetas River produced 11 giants for the author, including a 17 1/2, 16 1/2 and two 15 1/2 pounders in about two hours.

area, but most parties had a great deal of success catching plenty of peacocks and some giants. Our trip was no exception.

The five anglers in our group caught hundreds of peacock bass during the week, 37 were over 12 pounds apiece. I was fortunate enough to catch 11 of the giants, including a 17 1/2, 16 1/2 and two 15 1/2 pounders in about two hours on the last morning. Each angler in our party caught peacock giants between 16 and 16 1/2 pounds.

The heaviest fish measured 32 inches in length and had a girth of 20-1/2 inches. I also took an 11 pound, 33 1/2 inch long suribim eintado, a sporty, striped catfish that strikes artificials and fights like a game fish. We averaged about 20 to 25 peacocks each day per boat, and in some areas, we had another 30 to 40 piranha to battle.

Scotty's was concentrating their efforts then in the state of Para. Dick Hayes and co-owner Morgan MacDonnell have fished the Amazon tributaries and lagoons within a 200-mile radius of Santarem and are now considering other bases within that area in which to run

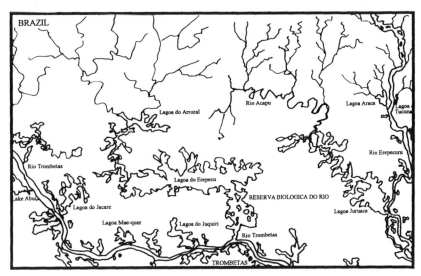

their operation. To find the very best peacock bass fishing in this remote area of the Amazon Rain Forest, you have to get to the small lagoons off of the moving water.

We fished the Trombetas and the Cumina River watersheds in Para, which is Brazil's second largest state; it's as large as Germany, France, the Benelux countries and Finland thrown in. The river originates in the highlands near the borders of Surinam and Guyana and flows south before linking up with the Amazon near Santarem.

The Trombetas River watershed and part of the Cumina River watershed encompass an ecological preserve where there is no commercial fishing allowed. Sport fishing here, although generally confined to catch-and-release, is also limited. The natives in this area do fish with hand-lines and canepoles, but their impact on the fishery is very minimal.

From the Amazon at Santarem, to the rapids at Acampamento, the entire length of the Rio Trombetas contains one large lagoon after another. Nearby, the Cumina or Erepecura River also offers several big lagoons and beautiful rapids. The two systems have a few waterfalls, as well as the numerous natural lakes and lagoons.

The falls and river sandbars to a lesser extent afford opportunities to wade fish some swift water areas that harbor payara up to 20 pounds or so. The surrounding land is forest-covered and those tributaries and lagoons to the north of the river have some hillsides adjacent to them.

F rom the Amazon at Santarem, to the rapids at Acampamento, the entire length of the Rio Trombetas contains one large lagoon after another.

Access, Facilities and Base of Operation

Air access to the area is good. The excellent flight from Miami to Belem aboard Varig takes about five hours. The transfers are all handled very capably and professionally with no hassles. You typically overnight in Belem, and the flight from Belem on to Port Trombetas on a Cruzeiro Airlines 737 jet is about another two hours.

The Varig flight schedule does change from time to time and may impact the itinerary. Most tour operators stay in close contact with the airline and destination and are aware of all changes of flights, operation location and facilities, as they occur.

Port Trombetas is located on the Trombetas River halfway between Belem and Manaus and northwest of the town of Santarem on the Amazon River. Port Trombetas is a modern mining community that's accessible only by airstrip, or by way of the Trombetas River from Santarem. There are no roads leading to this city of 3,000. The North River Mining Company is strip-mining bauxite (aluminum ore) at its mining operation about an hour's drive from town.

Rollin' On The River

Like most Brazilian sport fishing operations, Scotty's takes advantage of the distance between the various waterways by employing a live-aboard, double-decker riverboat. We had a choice of sleeping in hammocks or on mattresses placed on the floor on a partially-

The riverboat navigates the river at night or during the day while you're fishing to relocate near new fishing grounds.

covered top deck. The riverboat's lower deck had the headroom for a person of approximately 5'8" or less, so great care was taken not to bump our heads when walking about. The jungle riverboat offered a small bathroom and shower facilities as well as meals.

The riverboat did not have air-conditioning, and it's really not needed. You're fishing pretty much the full day, and you get back to the houseboat at around dark. The air cools down quickly at night, and it's very comfortable sleeping under the stars or under the roof on the second deck. There were no biting bugs!

The riverboat actually navigates the river at night to reposition for next-day fishing, or it moves about during the day while you're fishing to relocate at a different rendezvous area. That makes it easy to fish several lakes over a vast amount of water. The fishing boats we used were fairly slow, 19-foot aluminum craft with narrow beams and 25-h.p. motors. Distances between lakes can be anywhere from 10 minutes to 30 minutes or more depending on the area you're in.

An interesting sight along the main rivers are the boto porpoise with bright salmon pink bodies, the largest of several freshwater porpoises in the Amazon. I did a double-take when I first saw one of them swimming beside our boat. Along the shoreline jungle are howler monkeys, tropical birds, and numerous palm frond-thatched huts. Dugout canoes were parked beside huge Brazilian nut trees and vines that stretched skyward into branches of other trees.

Fishing Action Overview

The fishing action on the lagoons off the Trombetas and Cumina vary from lake to lake. Several lakes offer excellent fishing and very few of the lakes have any fishing pressure whatsoever. One of the interesting things that we found was that many of the lakes had small huts or houses on the different points. Dug-out canoes were a very common sight.

The only slight fishing pressure was subsistence fishing by locals who use natural bait and very light line in very shallow water. They generally caught only small fish, baitfish and other little varieties from four to 10 inches long. In effect, the pressure they put on the peacock fishery in this area of the Amazon is nonexistent as best as I can determine.

The water level of many lakes and lagoons fluctuate greatly, depending on the time of year. In early October we found the levels to be low. A few lakes off the Cumina River were even too shallow to fish, offering depths from one to three feet. Most of our better fishing was on cuts into the lagoons, and on points, feeding flats and saddles in those small bodies of water.

Several different locations are available to fish on the watershed unless it is too shallow. In certain areas up the Cumina River, there were extremely shallow waters and numerous sand bars that would limit travel, if the water was just six inches lower (than when we were there). The other thing that limits the travel are several check-in points for the biological reserve.

Expect to find good peacock bass fishing in many of the waters, and there are other opportunities for some great action. This watershed offers a huge variety of fish. We landed many piranha, including some giant five-pounders, and suribim, truly a sportfish that will hit a trolled lure or a cast lure and put up a tremendous fight.

The Cumina (Erepecuru) Watershed

Our expedition started at Port Trombetas. We traveled due east along the Rio Trombetas to the Cumina (also called Erepecuru) River. Then, we went north along the main branch of the Cumina to Lake Araca. This is the same water that Dick Ballard had taken a 15-pounder from just six weeks earlier. The big fish came off a point in Araca that we again checked out. When we got to the point, however, there were less than two feet of water in the entire area.

Lake Araca offers a sandy bottom with scattered grass patches throughout. Some beds were present in the shallow lagoon, although

The Cumina Watershed has productive boulders, undercut banks and rock outcroppings in a two or three mile stretch below the falls. We were able to catch about 20 small peacocks and other fish in the deeper water.

not occupied while we were there. The lake's topography is just extremely flat with only about two to four foot of water max during our early October visit. In Ballard's previous visit in August, the same areas had at least five or six feet of water.

During out trip however, the big lake was so shallow that we caught just a few small fish. When we were leaving the shallow lagoon, we discovered a deeper channel leading into the lake and experienced some excellent fishing. The channel was basically a wide canal with water four feet to seven or eight feet deep. The fish obviously were concentrated and we were able to catch many from that area as it connected the river to the lake. We caught peacocks up to about 10 pounds, some piranha and several suribim, including one 11-pounder.

We then fished Lake Tucunare, located on the other side of the Trombetas River, a short distance from Araca. Tucunare also was very shallow (two to three feet max) and flat. It had no deep water at all that October. We caught one fish in the deeper creek leading into the lake from the river.

South of Lake Tucunare is another lake that offered up a few small peacocks. From the river, we traveled through a small lake and into the larger Lake Jamuru. The fishing there was not exceptional. Nor was it that day in lakes further south along the watershed.

Our riverboat was moored that night at the Island of Maruim a mile or so up the Cumina River. The next day, we made the decision to go all the way up to the Cumina Falls. The waterfalls are as far as you can travel by boat. We had to pull the boat over several sandbars to get up to the falls. The falls themselves were not that productive, but the stretch just below them were full of piranha.

We caught about 20 small peacocks and other fish in the two- or three-mile stretch below the falls. Our lures fooled about 40 piranha which ran between three and five pounds apiece, and we had a couple of payara on but did not land them. We did land a few other different species, including some real colorful fish from the river below the falls.

The falls were about four to six feet high at the time we were there, but in that stretch are numerous huge boulders, undercut banks, rock outcropping everywhere and quite a bit of deep water. The water depth where we had nonstop action varied from three to 14 feet. We wound up the day fishing a little channel going into Lake Atacua. We had a fairly good day catching several peacocks, including one almost 11 pounds.

Our strategy for the following day was to fish lakes off the west side of the Cumina. From the junction of the Cumina and Trombetas, we followed the side channel north through the Lake de Tracua. From there, we traveled along a more defined channel all the way up to Salgada Lake.

Salgada is a very shallow lake in many places, but it does offer some neat areas with stickups. While we were fishing the areas, there was considerable fish movement. Lots of ducks flying around this particular lake were just one example of its intensive birdlife. The surroundings were unusual compared to the inhabitants on the shores of the other lakes in the area. Salgada was surrounded by ranch land and had a few pretty nice ranch houses and cattle grazing in the area. The fishing there was very slow.

We then went north to a horseshoe bend in the river and ducked into a small lagoon called Lake Sumba. We located the deep water channel and caught a 10 1/2 pounder. We only fished Lake Sumba about an hour before having to leave for the riverboat connection. It was late and got dark fast; our guide managed to hit three sandbars on the way back to our floating lodging.

The next day we explored the Cumina (Erepecuru) River arm further, specifically Lagoa (Lake) Juruaca and the Acapu River channel just above it. We were heading to Lake Acapu, but at a

A giant Rat-L-Trap cast while wading a shallow sand saddle attracted the attention of a 12 3/4 pounder.

"Ranger" station about two miles or so above Juruaca we received the bad news that Acapu and in fact the entire watershed above that check-in point was closed to sport fishing. We were prohibited from going further. In the river channel, we caught some nice size peacock bass and some large piranha. We fished Juruaca, trolled around some of its islands, but really didn't do well in that lake.

The Trombetas Watershed

We fished the upper Trombetas watershed on the very first full day of our trip. We first visited a big lake called Curuca-mirim, about 1 1/2 hours west of Port Trombetas by boat. We cast likely looking spots and caught a few mid-size peacocks, but my highlight that morning was a huge fish boiling up on my 7-inch long Jerkin' Sam topwater plug. It missed and never struck at other casts to the area.

We caught some decent-sized fish in the southern end of Curuca-mirim, including one about 10 pounds. Several of these came trolling the far southeastern corner of the lake with Rat-L-Traps and large minnow baits.

Others in our group of five anglers caught a few giants from the area. T. O. McLean caught one in the Curuca-mirim that weighed 13 1/2 pounds, but earlier that morning he had taken a 12 pounder and one that weighed 14 pounds from a small, unnamed lagoon behind Jamari Island between the Lake Curuca-mirim and Port Trombetas. The entrance to the small lake was located just southeast of the island.

The following day, we headed toward the Cumina watershed. Since I had only caught four big peacocks between 8 1/2 and 11 pounds in the first four days (the big fish of each day), we decided to look for the true giants (those over 15 pounds) again in the Trombetas watershed. While we slept on the riverboat, it motored from the Cumina River anchorage back to the Rio Trombetas past Port Trombetas and then into the upper Trombetas area. We got up the next morning after traveling all night in a storm and found ourselves anchored at the mouth of Lake Tapagem Grande.

From there, we boarded our boats and went north through a side channel to Lake Abui. We spent probably the first hour and a half in unproductive water, catching only one or two small peacocks. We were trolling a point on the western end of the lake when Dick caught our boat's first true giant, a 16-pounder.

After that pleasant experience, we discovered a couple of different things. We trolled another cove and along a very sandy point which ran toward a little island about 200 yards off the land point. As we motored past the underwater extension from the point over a long, narrow saddle, we both commented on what a typically-productive structure this saddle looked like.

The saddle had deep water on the near side and relatively deep water on the backside. We stopped our trolling pass, made casts to the deep water and Ballard had on a big fish. Before he had landed the 12 pounder, I had a bigger fish on. My fish slammed a Super Trap and was weighed at the boat prior to being released. It was 12 3/4 pounds.

We decided then to get out of the boat, wade out on the shallow sand saddle, where I caught another, even bigger fish, a 14 pounder. Waters beside the sandy saddle were relatively clear of weeds and other aquatic vegetation. I had two more huge peacocks hooked on that Super Trap, but each pulled off before being landed and weighed. I did land two more, each just under 10 pounds, and Ballard another mid-size peacock, before we moved on to a flat area about five feet deep adjacent to several acres of shallow, flooded brush.

We decided to try a fast trolling method over the flat using giant topwater lures. This same technique had been successful for Ballard while on Venezuela's Casiquiare River and lagoons. We began trolling topwater plugs in the bay in Lake Abui, and this feeding flat provided our best action on giant peacocks.

Such places can be, as in any fishing, hot or cold. The one that we came across was hot. It remained hot the one full day and last half day we had to fish it. Ballard and I caught many of our 12-pound-plus fish within a couple hundred yard stretch. In fact, on the final morning, we caught 32 peacocks averaging around 10 pounds each.

The Madeira Watershed

The only float plane operation currently in South America is owned and operated by Luis Brown and his River Plate Wings company. With a couple of float planes based out of Manaus, his clients are able to access the very best peacock fisheries in Brazil. And, he's got some great watersheds to fish that others with various forms of transportation can't reach.

I recently visited one of his "southern fisheries." From my limited experience in Brazil (two other trips) I have to call the Madeira River watershed the very best that I've experienced. The peacocks in some of the more remote tributaries there were plentiful, and there were many giant fish too. Everyone in my group consistently caught peacocks that averaged over 7 pounds each!

Our small group consisted of U.S. tour booking agents Tom Spang of Frontiers and Dick Ballard of Fishing Adventures, along with avid peacock bass specialists Tom Nash of Birmingham, Alabama and T.O. McLean of Odessa, Texas and husband/wife duo Bill and Gail Kavanaugh, currently of Montevideo, Uruguay. Everyone caught lots of fish in the numerous small lagoons off the larger rivers. We found the most action that week at the "bocas" or mouths of the long, narrow lagoons which were filled with flooded timber such as stumps, brushpiles, laydowns and massive rotten trunks. It was a mean place to try to land a giant peacock, but everyone did.

Obviously, some giants weren't landed. In fact, we each probably lost 15 fish per day. Our group's daily individual catch averaged about 20 to 25 fish and most of us probably could count another 30 to 50 strikes, follows and boils that didn't result in a solid hook up. Such averages are impressive for a peacock fishery.

Our group caught and released eight peacocks over 14 pounds each. Other fish averaged about 7 pounds each. I was fortunate to land the two largest of the week, "twins" weighing 17 1/2 pounds each, on giant topwater plugs. Ballard out-battled a giant that pushed our certified scales to 17 1/4 pounds. He, like most of us, employed large surface lures for the brown-black waters which had clarity averaging about two feet. Most of the peacock were taken casting the large baits, but a few hit a trolled lure.

Spang, a master flyfisherman on his first peacock bass angling trip, used a long (No. 9) wand and a variety of streamers to land numerous fish up to 10 pounds. He also caught and released a 14-pounder after casting a large topwater plug in "one of his weaker moments." He and float plane pilot Reverend Bennie DeMarchant compared fly fishing techniques on the water. ''Pastor Bennie'', who has fished Amazon jungle rivers all over Brazil for 20-some years, utilized short roll casts to entice numerous strikes in the dense flooded jungles of the Maderinha River, part of the Madeira (also spelled Mederia on some maps) watershed.

After wearing ourselves out on the peacocks each day, we returned to the most comfortable fishing camp that I've been to. Huge two-man floor tents with spring beds, table and chair made our accommodations clean and a pleasant camping experience. A 7kV 24-hour generator to keep our drinks and food cold and tarpaulins over the supper table and kitchen area added to the comfort.

Brown's camping operation handles eight anglers (he calls them ''rods'') comfortably. The four tents have individual showers and flushing toilets. Also at the camp is a radio for contact with Manaus, and all the guides have emergency kits which hold a VHF radio, flares, smoke signals, potable water pills and a medical kit.

Luis' staff was very helpful and my guide Ivon was probably the best overall peacock guide that I've ever fished with; there's been a bunch that I've had to ''train.'' The boats and 25 hp outboards were all in great shape. Not once during the week did my guide have the cowling off the outboard, and that's rare in South America.

The amiable host has set a goal for his operation to provide a very comfortable camp, far away from commercial fishing pressure and populations in general. If the fishing is not good on the tributary where his temporary camp is located, he will simply pick it up and move. The flexibility of the camp, boats and even float planes allows Brown to fish a large variety of rivers in the Amazon.

Brown sets up camp in remote stretches of several rivers. In September and October, he is usually fishing south of Manaus. One area southeast of the Madeira River has beautiful sandbars and lagoons. Another fishery in the Igapoacu Maderinha area is southwest of Manaus and provides excellent fishing through early November.

Both river areas south of Manaus offer dark water lagoons. The southeast lagoons tend to be black water, and the rivers in that region are clearer than waters in other areas, according to Brown. The southwest river waters are not as clear and the lagoons are a black/brown mixture. Both areas are difficult for commercial fishermen to access. The Maderinha has numerous large rocks at its mouth, and large vessels seldom navigate through them. The barrier on the Madeira is low water levels prior to getting into deeper waters near the headwaters.

Chapter 7

UATUMA, TUCURUI AND OTHER BRAZILIAN ACTION

Great fishing exists in the remote reaches of Brazil

In Brazil, the peacock bass, or tucunare, is found only in the Amazon Basin, which is probably 75 percent of the country. Tributaries pour in from remote reaches north and south. The Basin, which parallels the equator over its length, is not the most populous part of the country, but it is not just wilderness.

The population centers of Manaus, about 1,000 miles inland, and Belem (each with over one million people) offer resort hotels and, unfortunately, intensive commercial fishing that takes a toll on the peacock fishery. For productive angling, you have to fish at least two hours by boat away from areas worked by the commercial fishermen. Local subsistence fishing seems to have little impact.

The Amazon Basin includes the states of Mato Grosso, Amazones, Para (which is the state that I fished), Tocantins, Goias and a couple of smaller ones. Brazil has 26 states, most of which offer some great fishing opportunities, but fishing many of them away from the populated southeast coast is difficult logistically. In remote parts of Brazil, there is little in the way of infrastructure.

Para's Giant Impoundment

The huge Tucurui Reservoir and Dam backing up the Tocantins River and the Araguaia River is about 200 miles south, southwest of Belem. Most fishing operations base themselves out of the town of Tucurui in the state of Para, but with the aid of a riverboat have access to the upper end of the lake.

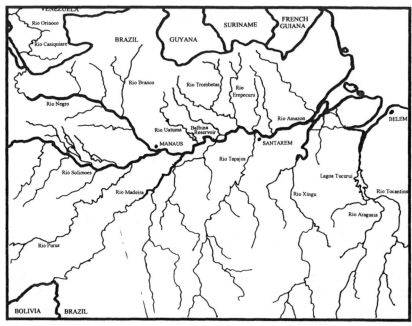

   This is a huge power-generating reservoir, very much like Guri Lake in Venezuela. There are a lot of residents in this area, however. When they built the dam, migrants came in from all over the northeast which is the driest, most impoverished part of Brazil. When the dam across the Tocantins River was finished, the need for a work force diminished and a lot of people simply stuck around. The unemployed work force at Tucurui had no place to go, so the people try to eke out a subsistence.

   As a result, there is considerable commercial fishing around the Tucurui dam. To get to the good peacock fishing, you have to boat 10 or 15 miles farther up the 100-mile long reservoir. The fishing there can be very good for numbers of peacock and for some giant peacocks, according to the Walkers who run the Amazon Mission Organization.

   Richard, Boyd and Winston Walker have been doing missionary work in the basin for more than 20 years and have recently begun operating peacock bass trips. They are intimately familiar with the fishing resources throughout the entire Amazon watershed and have selected the upper end of Lake Tucurui and its headwaters, the Rio Araguaia and Rio Tocantins, as one of two prime Brazilian spots in

B *razilian guides most frequently use 16-foot aluminum boats with 25 to 45-hp outboards.*

which to focus. They have taken peacocks to 16 pounds from those waters, as well as huge payara (primarily below the Tucurui dam). They utilize a riverboat based out of the village of Maraba (at the upper end of the reservoir) to make excursions upstream. Guided fishing is from 16-foot aluminum boats with 25 to 45 hp outboards and swivel seats. May through October are the prime fishing months in this region and the typical itinerary covers eight or nine days.

Westward Along The Amazon

The fishing along the Amazon Basin within a 200-mile radius of Santarem is generally good, but you have to get off the big rivers and into the small lagoons to find it; the peacocks don't hang out in the fast moving water. The Tapajos River south of Santarem is an area that currently offers poor fishing due to mercury poisoning. There are many lakes in the Obidos and Oriximina region, however, that have reportedly very good fishing.

A few fishing tour promoters offer programs in the Amazon further upstream, past Manaus off the huge Rio Negro stem of the Amazon. Some tour operators have explored tributaries north of Barcelos (off the Rio Negro). Others have looked at another area southwest of Manaus, which encompasses the tributaries of the Negro River and the Solimoes River and their lagoons. Operation competition is good for all most Brazilians believe, because it helps the Amazon Basin to become known as a peacock destination.

Another peacock place of importance is the Guapore River, located on the border of Bolivia in the Brazilian state of Rondonia. There is a lodge at Pinateras and flights into the town of Delinia. The problem for travelers from the states is that the only access is from southern Brazil, a long distance from Miami. The peacock bass fishing is reported very good, but you have to run a long distance to fish the best spots. The fishing there for payara is also good, particularly around the river's rapids.

Uatuma River Offerings

The Uatuma River, a tributary of the mighty Amazon and Rio Negro rivers in the Manaus region, is now one of the hotbeds of peacock activity in Brazil. It lies about half way between Santarem and Manaus and offers miles of clean, white sandy beaches and islands during the dry season. It also offers huge peacock bass. Walker's Amazon Mission Organization offers packages to this area from September to mid-December. They utilize a houseboat for maximum flexibility and area coverage.

The rainy season here, starting in December, changes the terrain and the fishing. Water levels rise some 25 to 40 feet cresting normally in June. A month or two later, much lower rivers in the area offer excellent peacock fishing once again. In fact, the low-water period of September may provide the best fishing of the year. By then, waters are clear, and the best fishing generally lasts through October. "Generally," being the key word. Weather patterns do change, and the peak season can be later, or sporadic during the summer and fall.

There are numerous 15 to 20 pound fish in the Uatuma and quite possibly one that could oust the current IGFA all-tackle world record peacock of 26 pounds, 8 ounces. Some monsters weighing nearly 25 pounds have been reported. There are reports of even larger peacocks in the area, according to Dr. Gilberto Fernandes, an IGFA representative in Manaus. He has reportedly weighed peacocks of nearly 30 pounds and has seen even larger commercially-caught fish.

The Walker's Uatuma fishing package also includes the Jatapu River and the upper Balbina Lake, which is located on the Uatuma River. Fishing pressure on the Balbina is nil, according to Dick Ballard who has explored the area with the Walkers. He has seen peacocks up to 20 pounds taken from the reservoir. The Jatapu, a tributary of the Uatuma/Amazon, yielded a 8-pound line class IGFA record in September of 1992. The fish caught by Fernandes weighed 20 pounds, 3 ounces.

T here are numerous 15 to 20 pound fish in the Uatuma and quite possibly one that could oust the current IGFA all-tackle world record peacock of 26 pounds, 8 ounces.

Mato Grosso Operations

There are excellent peacock waters all over the northern half of Brazil, and those far up (south) the Araguaia are no exception. Scotty's Sport Fishing has an operation called the Kuryala Fishing Lodge in the state of Mato Grosso southeast of Trombetas near the confluence of the Araguaia River and Rio Das Mortes that provides excellent peacock action. Located on a picturesque bluff overlooking the Araguaia River, the lodge is fronted by beaches of sand.

Directly in front of the lodge is Bananal Island, the largest river island in the world formed by the surrounding waters of the east and west branches of the Araguaia River. The lodge is slightly south of the small river port town of Sao Felix do Aqaguaia.

"The logistics for getting to the lodge is not easy," explains Hayes. "You have to fly all the way from the states to Rio De Janeiro and then back to the capital, Brasilia, spend the night in Brasilia, and then hop on a 44-passenger plane. The fishing is worth it, though."

The best fishing times in the southern region of the Amazon Basin of Brazil are influenced by a seasonal rain pattern and water level variations which is quite different from the watershed in the mid or northern parts of the Amazon Basin. Prime fishing months are from the latter part of April until the first of December each year. In the upper and mid Amazon areas, where dozens of major tributaries feed the huge river, the best fishing season, normally from September until mid-December.

Near the confluence of the Araguaia River and Rio Das Mortes River, there are several lakes which offer big numbers of peacock bass, but trophies over 12 pounds are scarce, according to Hayes. A number of the lakes near the lodge can be reached in 20 minutes to one hour. Some excellent land-locked lakes are also within a short walking distance of the river channels. In the upper lakes area there is excellent peacock bass fishing both in terms of numbers and size.

The Rio Das Mortes

The Rio Das Mortes offers several lagoons, lakes and waterways where two partners in a boat can catch 100 peacocks a day and have a chance at bigger fish. There are also two good lakes within the lodge property, which can be reached by jeep in a few minutes. Fishing from the sandy beaches of land-locked lakes offers an interesting change of pace.

For the "explorers", a houseboat provides live-aboard accommodations while moving about fishing areas in mid-river locations during the low water period of the season, from mid-July onward. As the river level drops, the houseboat can only navigate upstream a short distance. However, it is still possible to reach the upper river lakes, ponds and waterways in the fishing boats by traveling from an hour and a half to two hours even late in the season.

The houseboat is normally used to reach the upper river's best fishing locations during May, June and July. This is the time of year that the houseboat can easily travel up the Rio Das Mortes River to a large area of numerous channels, lakes, ponds and islands. Traveling up to this particular area is generally done at night so that valuable daytime fishing is not wasted.

Fishing can be good in the early morning times close to where the houseboat anchors for the night on sandy beach islands and extensive

R io Das Mortes peacocks have four or five gray bars on their sides instead of the familiar three black vertical bars common to most peacock bass around the world.

sand bars along the main river. Fishing is generally done in the shallower channels in and around sand banks. In the early hours of the day, there is considerable movement of fish in the very clear waters as they seek concentrations of baitfish. Fishing from the banks of these channels, or wading out to cast, often puts the fishermen into schools of fish.

Gray-Bar Peacock Species

The peacocks you catch here, some 80 miles south of the massive Tucurui Reservoir, may look a little different from those you are used to seeing. The peacock sub-species available here are indeed very different, according to those who have caught them. Rio Das Mortes peacocks have four or five gray bars on their sides instead of the familiar three black vertical bars common to most peacock bass around the world.

The fishing in this area is best in the lagoons that range in depth from five to seven feet. Often, you can easily a deep-running lure in those clear waters. Very little bottom structure exists in the dishpan-type lagoons. Along the fringes, you might find trees or brush.

Suribim, a strikingly-patterned catfish that can exceed 150 pounds, is one example of the unique variety of fish in the rivers and lagoons of Brazil.

The backwaters behind the sand banks and below the islands also offer good early morning fishing to those wading quietly through the shallows.   During the night, a variety of gamefish come into the shallows to escape giant predatory fish in the depths.   In the backwaters, you can catch peacock.

Variety Abounds

You will find a big variety of fish in the rivers and lagoons of Brazil. Besides peacocks, you may tangle with aruana, a tarpon-like fish with a "clubby" tail that grows to 25 pounds; pescada, which look like drum and grow to 20 pounds; pacu, a bluegill-like fish that runs to 20 pounds in moving waters; matrincha, a shad-like fish indigenous to Brazil that grows to 12 pounds; several kinds of piranha (the red head, the silver and the black, among others); corvina; payara; suribim, which can exceed 150 pounds; bicuda; and an occasional golden-colored tabarana.

While there are hundreds, make that thousands of good spots for catching peacocks in the Amazonas watershed, the major problem to fishermen can be the water levels. Low water periods in the rivers of

Brazil vary, even those in the same state. When the water levels are high, fishing is much tougher; the fish are back in the jungle. When the conditions are such, clients should reschedule their trip for a later date. Most responsible tour operators let people know ahead of time that conditions may not be ideal.

Manaus offers a good jumping off point for much of the Amazon fishing, and reaching Manaus is not a problem, thanks to regular air service from the U.S. There are weekly nonstop flights on Varig (about 4 3/4 hours) from Miami. But you had better go with a fishing tour operator!

Exploring Brazil On Your Own

There are no marinas, fishing resorts, fish camps, boat rental places, or sport fishing guides in the interior of Brazil. For anglers to go into the Amazon Basin and fish anywhere is very difficult. If they don't speak Portuguese and have access to a boat, it would be

ENGLISH	PORTUGUESE	PHONETIC PRONUNCIATION
Good morning	Bom dia	Bom dee-ah
Good afternoon	Boa tarde	Boah tar-de
Good evening/night	Boa noite	Boah nochee
Thank you	Obrigado	Oh-bree-gahdoh
You're welcome	De nada	Day nah-dah
Closer	Mas perto	Mahs pear-toh
Farther away	Mas longe	Mahs lown-gee
Slow down	Devagar	Day vahgar
Faster	Mas rapido	Mahs rah-peedoe
Hurry up	Rapidinho	Rah-pee-dee-nho
Now	Agora	Ah-gore-ah
Today	Hoje	Oh-gee
Yesterday	Ontem	Own-teng
Tomorrow	Amanha	Ah-mah-nha
Shore or bank	Costa	Coe-stah
Another place	Outro lugar	Oh-true loo-gar
Return	Voltar	Volt-are
Fish	Peixe	Pay-she
Peacock bass	Tucunare	Too-coon-are-a
Payara	Peixe cachorro	Pay-she cah-shore-oh
Boat	Barco	Bar-coe
Paddle	Remo	Rey-mow
Rod	Vara	Var-ah

practically impossible. Hayes, who speaks Portuguese fluently, had difficulty in finding a boat most everywhere he has visited. At most locations, it takes a "local" three or four days to line up a craft.

The different language may pose problems. The guides do not speak English for the most part, although they may know a few words. Portuguese is similar to Spanish but there could be communication problems. An interpreter typically accompanies each group, so communication during transfers around hotels and aboard a riverboat is not a problem. Most of the tour operations will have a tip sheet with key Portuguese words to help the angler communicate with the guide.

Scotty's Sport Fishing suggests the words and phrases in the chart on the previous page may be helpful to know. Concerning pronunciation, know that consonants are spoken roughly the same in Portuguese as in English. The vowels tend to give Americans the most trouble. A, E, I, O and U are pronounced phonetically as if they are Ah, Eh, EE, Oh and Oo, respectively.

Chapter 8

THE COLOMBIA/PANAMA CONNECTION

For the biggest, smallest and most remote populations

Both Colombia and Panama offer excellent peacock bass fishing, and the Guyanas on the northern coast of South America are real "sleepers". The political climate may or may not be right for a visit to some of these countries at any given time. Some tour operators do schedule trips to Colombia and are optimistic about personal safety and hassle-free travel. Other fishing tour promoters remain more cautious.

Panama is currently promoting travel to sportsmen, and my recent trip confirmed a very safe, pleasant atmosphere in the country.

Colombia's Matevini River Records

Colombia has outstanding fishing for peacock bass in their Llanos region near the eastern border. The headwaters of Brazil's Amazon River are born in Colombia. Reports of peacocks to 40 pounds have surfaced from time to time, and the existing world record did come from this country.

Booking fishing trips to the country may be frustrating. Some of the few fishing camps are currently closed and have canceled their seasons because of "trouble". While on the rivers, you might expect an altercation from "head hunters" as you coast around each bend. You might expect piranhas to jump over the boat's gunwale to snip at your flesh, but neither is a possibility. Nor is the dense jungle likely to be threatening. Any ''trouble'' may be associated with the country's illegal drug trade.

In Colombia, peacock fishing in the Matevini River near the border of Venezuela and Colombia between San Fernando and Port Ayacucho is excellent. In fact, the current world record peacock, caught by Dr. Rod Neubert, came from the Matevini. The lagoons off the river are six to ten feet deep with an average visibility of two to three feet. There are two or three very clear lagoons that are exceptions, however, according to avid peacock angler T. O. McLean of Odessa, Texas.

''The first week I was there I caught eight over 20 pounds,'' he says. ''That was in 1982. My partner caught eight over 20 pounds in just one afternoon. He hadn't caught any big ones all week.''

The largest peacock that McLean caught was a 24-pounder, which would have held the world record for a few days. Neubert caught his 26 1/2 pounder that same week.

''Shortly after that, the government of Colombia stopped anglers from going in there because of drug trafficking risks,'' says McLean. ''So the area hasn't been fished much since 1983. I'm hoping to again get permission to go in there!''

Other Colombian Tributaries

McLean also fished another one of the Colombian river tributaries that flowed into Venezuela. In a no-name lagoon off of it, fishing was excellent. The water in this lagoon was a little clearer than that in most of the other lagoons. The visibility was about three feet with a maximum depth of 10 to 12 feet.

He and his partner were the first ones to ever go to that lagoon, according to their Indian guide. To access the ''deep water'' lagoon, the men had to boat through a shallow creek for several miles and even pull the boat across shoals that extended for about three-quarters of a mile. McLean went into that secret spot four times and caught all the peacocks, big piranha, and suribim that he could handle.

''Throw a Rat-L-Trap against the bank near the tree roots and brush, and you could catch a butterfly peacock on every cast,'' he says. ''But in the middle, you catch the big ones. While the giant peacocks did exist, I never did catch one over 20 pounds. I caught several between 18 and 19 1/2 pounds, however.''

Most international flights to Colombia go through Bogota, a city of over two million inhabitants. The loftiest capital city in the world

C olombia has some outstanding fishing for giant peacock bass, however, booking a trip to the country can be frustrating.

lies only a few hundred miles north of the Equator in a high, wide Andean Valley at 8,600 feet elevation. The rugged mountains which have roadways crossing at over 12,000 feet begin at the city's edge. Flights to ''peacock land'' from the capital often connect at the town of Villavicenzio, east of Bogota at the foot of the Andes.

Vaupes River Lagoons

McLean has flown the route in the past and fished the Apaporis River in the southeastern part of Colombia. The area, about three hours from the Brazilian border, also consists of the Vaupes River which ultimately flows into Brazil's Rio Negro. Some call the Vaupes lagoons the most beautiful and unique string offering the finest bass fishing in the world.

The connection point for the Vaupes is Miraflores, which lies about 1-1/2 hours by air southeast of Villavicenzio. A dirt and grass airstrip, built by the U.S. Rubber Company years ago for exporting rubber, provides access to this part of the jungle. The village of Little Miraflores is a couple of rows of houses and huts around the airstrip, a two-hour boat ride from the Vaupes River and the El Dorado Lakes. The peacock fishing in the Vaupes and its lagoons used to be fairly good, according to McLean, but the average size of peacocks was small. A 10-pounder would be a good fish. The drug traffic closed down that fishing also, according to the avid angler.

Another excellent river that reportedly yields giant peacocks is Colombia's Bita River. According to my sources, most locations in

Colombia offer 15 to 20 peacocks per person each day and a 15-pound-plus giant over the typical four-day trip.

When it rains in the Colombian jungle, it may pour buckets for two days straight, then quit for a few hours, and continue once again for another two days. Runoff from the flooded jungle after the storms is usually slow. Peacocks that disperse from the rain-swollen rivers into the jungle to feed will usually return to more accessible (by fishermen) spots later, when rains cease and water levels subside.

At the end of the rainy season, many rivers are 20 to 30 feet higher than in the dry season. Butterflies are everywhere and orchids cover the trees in some areas. Given the weather options, the dry season, November to March in the eastern part of Colombia, usually provides the best fishing.

As the water level drops after the rainy season, it is often so rapidly that peacocks are trapped in ponds and oft-times landlocked lagoons off the tributary channels. A hike through the dense jungle for two or three miles might bring you to a 40-acre pool of hungry fish. The fish may be thrashing around the shallow potholes in fantastic numbers. Some anglers have reported catching 50 peacocks in a row and stopping their count at 200!

Panama's Huge Gatun Lake

Peacocks are very abundant in the beautiful Lake Gatun in Panama, but most of the fish are very small, one-half to two pounds. The 50 mile long Panama Canal goes right through the big, 163.4-square-mile lake. The impoundment, surrounded by tropical rain forest jungle, is the third largest reservoir in the world and provides the water for the passage of 40 ships a day (each uses 54 million gallons).

Lake Gatun, with its 1,090 miles of shoreline, was created in 1914 on the northern side of the canal by the damming of the Chagres River to flood the hills inside the Caribbean Coastal Ridge. It was needed to provide the enormous amount of water needed to operate the locks at the Atlantic Ocean end of the painstakingly-dug canal.

The country's capital city of well over one million population is located on the Pacific Ocean canal end, about one hour away from the lake. The drive from Panama City is over good highways and twisting country roads through beautiful, rolling hillside with scattered palms, oaks, banana trees, bamboo and papaya growing in rich soil, red clay, and occasional rocks.

*P*eacocks are very abundant in the beautiful Lake Gatun in Panama, but most of the fish are very small, one-half to two pounds.

The lake initially had a native fish community consisting entirely of species with a riverine origin. As one biologist put it, "the fishery was characterized by the notable absence of a top level predator." Enter the peacock bass or as the locals commonly refer to them, the "tucunare" or "sargento". Some reports of the initial stocking of Lake Gatun claim the date was in the early 1950s. Most, however, say the introduction occurred accidentally in 1964 when a small privately-owned pond full of butterfly peacocks from Guyana overflowed into the Chagres.

The World's Only Over-Population

After the unplanned introduction, the peacock fishery exploded as the fish overpopulated. Consequently, this is not a catch-and-release fishery, as are others south of the U.S. In fact, the lake is so crowded with peacocks, the Panama fishery officials request heavy harvesting and that no bass be returned to the lake. After the introduction, biologists have noted that native forage fish populations (and both tarpon and snook) have decreased.

The greenish-clear waters of Gatun are interesting. The fairly stable water temperature varies from about 82.4 degrees to 86.4 degrees. Floating water hyacinths and duckweed are relatively abundant, and many large bays are filled with giant flooded trees and stumps and hydrilla weedbeds.

Barro Colorado, one of the largest islands in the lake is home to a Smithsonian research station. Numerous other islands around the lake contain a rich biodiversity of birds and animals as well. There are countless stumps and snags grown up over the years prior to impoundment. Local markers and navigational buoys left by the U.S. Coast Guard try to keep boaters out of trouble, but you have to leave the marked channel to catch fish.

The lake's maximum depth is 95 feet and the average is about 41 feet. The depths of Gatun near the 80-foot deep channel also include a 100-year old French train, engine and 30 cars still on the tracks. Amongst the flooded stumps are at least two towns, pieces of 19th century canal-digging equipment and several sunken ships.

Gatun's Size and Quantity

Gatun is a small peacock bass paradise. You can expect 60 to 150 peacocks per boat each day (year-around), but very few will nose three or four pounds. Fish in the six- or seven-pound class here are worth bragging about. The primary variety of peacock in Gatun is the butterfly, the smaller member of the peacock Cichla genus.

Several anglers have reported catching up to 200 per boat on a good day at Gatun. The lake is the best place in the world to catch and keep big numbers of peacocks. As I said, biologists even urge harvesting of the numerous peacock bass since the lake's population is underfished. About 15 to 20 boats fish the lake each weekend day. During the week, only five of these boats ply these waters.

Gatun Lake has produced excellent fishing for numbers of peacock almost from day one, but the opportunity was little known outside of Panama. The only serious fishermen to fish artificials on the giant lake have been Panama Canal employees and U.S. government personnel. Most local anglers and guides are content with fishing one- to two-inch long silver/white minnows called "sardines" from an anchored boat.

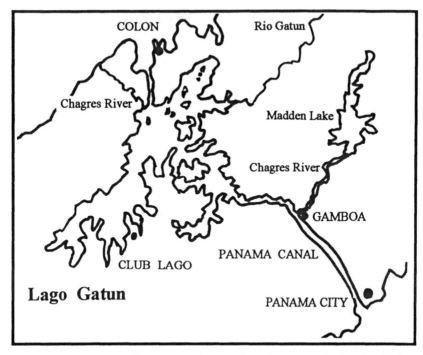

Lure tossers on Gatun employ surface lures, white bucktail jigs and spoons around the weedbeds. Peacocks tend to concentrate around points near submerged trees and stumps near hydrilla beds where they can forage and then return to the bases of deep water trees. Spoon jigging the deep trees for large peacocks can be productive, and slow trolling for numbers of peacocks can be effective.

I fished the lake in late April from a wide, 16-foot aluminum boat with guide Cholo Trejos and found the peacocks to be very cooperative. In about six hours of fishing, Trejos and I caught about 35 peacocks each. He was using the live sardines while I was tossing a small Jerkin' Sam topwater bait. The small peacocks would come up and pounce on the wood plug as it was softly twitched near cover. We caught about a dozen peacocks between 1 1/2 and 2 1/2 pounds, while the rest were smaller.

Top Spots and Facilities

Not all fish in the lake are small. According to Trejos, a guide on Gatun for the last eight years, the lake record peacock stands at 9 1/2 pounds. He says that while the early morning hours provide

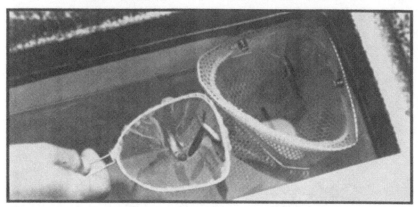

*M*ost local anglers and guides use one or two-inch long silver/white minnows called "sardines" and fish from an anchored boat.

excellent catches, most of the five-pound or better peacocks are taken in the late afternoon, between 5 and 7 p.m. Specific spots to look on Gatun for larger peacocks are La Garter, La Garterita and Escobal cove areas.

Twenty pound snook also swim in Lake Gatun and 60 to 80 pound tarpon are present in even greater numbers, but light tackle anglers seldom land them in the structure-filled impoundment. There is some subsistence fishing of peacocks, but that has had little effect on the sport fishing. Sources that have been keeping track of such things since 1967 report about 40 tons of peacocks are taken by these people each year.

There are a couple of marinas on the lake, one at Chagres River and another at Club Lago resort on a more remote portion of Gatun near the town of Arenosa. I fished out of both, and the better fishing appears to be around the latter which is well away from the canal traffic.

There is a crumbling concrete ramp for public launching in the small native village of Gamboa at the southern tip of the lake. From Gamboa, it's a short cruise past small white stone towers (set up for channel alignment) through the thick tropical jungle to the massive lake. In the main channel of the canal, you may see submarines, battle ships or cargo ships moving slowly by.

Panama's Two Other Lakes

There are two other lakes in Panama that offer peacock bass fishing, Las Cumbres Lake and Lago Alajuela. Alajuela, also commonly called Madden Lake, is located on the headwaters of the Chagres River. It was created in 1935 as a reservoir above Lake Gatun to better control the water needs of the lower lake. The residents around the lake are more dense on Alajuela and the fishing pressure, if you can call it that, is greater. One study found 2.3 boats per square mile on Alajuela and about half that on Gatun.

Alajuela is a 19.2 square mile lake with 155 miles of shoreline. It has an average depth of 53 feet and maximum depth of 157 feet. Its water temperatures vary more than Gatun's. Summer temps are 88 degrees while it cools down to 81 degrees in the so-called "winter" months. The lake is actually more fertile than Gatun, but the peacocks in Alajuela are generally smaller. The most plausible explanation for that is that Gatun has a substantial forage base of sardines that have come through the locks from the sea.

Timing The Bite

The very best fishing in all three of the lakes, according to Archie Kirchman of Nattur Panama, is near the end of the dry season in April. The lower lake levels means bigger fish. The dry season starts in December and many of the peacocks move into the sardine-laden tributaries to spawn during February or March. High winds characterize much of the dry season from December through April, but these months offer the best fishing. The rainy season in Panama is normally from May/June through October/November, and the fishing can also be good then.

The Panama Tourist Office is quick to point out that the country's name Panama means "abundance of fish", and what I found on Lake Gatun seems to confirm it. Accessing Panama City is by jet non-stop from Miami. American Airlines (1-800-433-7300) offers a comfortable flight with connecting flights throughout the U.S., and I recommend that carrier to those visiting Panama. For information on the peacock fishing in Gatun Lake, contact Club Lago, c/o Archibaldo Kirchman, Nattur Panama, PO Box 5068, Balboa Ancon, Panama or phone (507)25-7325.

The Guyanas Promise

The small South American countries of Guyana and Suriname may hold great promise for peacock fishing someday; but for now, they are not easy travel options. The butterfly peacock's native range is in the lowlands of the western Guianas, basically from the Essequibo River in Guyana to the Marowijne River on the border of Suriname and French Guiana.

The jungle rivers in Guyana's lowlands should be outstanding, but getting there and accessing them seems to be almost impossible. Peacocks in the Essequibo River system are the smaller butterfly species. Peacock bass also inhabit man-made irrigation trenches near Georgetown, Guyana, but sources state the fish are relatively small. They usually weigh between three and five pounds, although specimens have been known to scale up to eight pounds there.

In Suriname, formerly Dutch Guiana, most of the river drainages are independent. The coastal lowlands are flat and marshy with a band of savannas, while the interior is primarily rain forest. Seasonal flooding occurs during two rainy seasons (December to February and April to July) in the savanna areas, while the higher drainages are comprised of numerous rapids.

The peacocks inhabit the Suriname, Marowijne, Saramacca, Nickerie, and Carantijn River systems. They can also be found in Lake Brokopondomeer, which is part of the Suriname River system, and Gran River above the country's only large lake. The speckled peacock has been found in the Branco River drainage in Guyana, but those fish were thought to have been imported from Brazil for fish culture projects and released into area rivers.

Chapter 9

HAWAII'S TENACIOUS TUCUNARE

Two scenic Pacific islands offer peacock action

Coconut palms, fields of blowing sugar cane and beautiful mountain peaks surround the United States' most unique peacock bass fishery. You'll be impressed with the Hawaiian waters' scenery and healthy peacock populations. And the action is just 2,400 miles from the mainland!

In Hawaii, the peacock bass is called "tucunare" or "tuc" for short. It was imported to Kauai, the islands' test site from Guyana (formerly called British Guiana), South America in 1957. Butterfly peacocks -- the smaller of the species -- were introduced to many Hawaii freshwater reservoirs in 1966 after a comprehensive evaluation by fishery biologist William S. Devick. He concluded that peacock bass tended to complement the existing largemouth bass fishery rather than compete with it. His conclusion was based on differing spawning seasons, distinctive albeit overlapping food habits, and somewhat different habitat preferences.

Since the introduction, peacock bass have become the basis of an important freshwater sportfishery. The fish has prospered and is now widespread. The state-wide Hawaii Freshwater Fishing Association (HFFA) even featured a leaping peacock bass as the center piece of its emblem.

The Hawaiian archipelago consists of over 130 islands and reefs stretching across 1,500 miles of Pacific Ocean. Of the six major Hawaiian islands, Kauai, Oahu, Maui, Hawaii, Lanai and Molokai, peacocks are now found on all but the latter two. They are generally

found in the larger reservoirs on those four islands. While the fish average about 2 to 3 pounds, the state record, caught by Dean Bailey, is 8 pounds, 13 ounces. It was taken from Tanaka Pond on the island of Kauai in 1982. Naturally, there are reports of larger peacocks being caught (and not certified for a record) in Hawaiian waters.

The terrain of the islands is beautiful and unique. Streams on the leeward slopes are mostly intermittent, while the windward slopes are often characterized by cliffs and valleys with high annual rainfall and many perennial streams. Despite the abundance of freshwater and hundreds of streams, the only freshwater fishes native to Hawaii are four gobies and an eleotrid, collectively known as 'o'opu.

There are only five small natural lakes in Hawaii, but there are almost 300 freshwater reservoirs that range up to 1,000 surface acres in size. The impoundments are generally home to the peacock and largemouth bass. Various other fish species from around the world have been introduced into reservoir and stream habitats, such as rainbow trout on Kauai, smallmouth bass on Oahu and Kauai, and bluegill statewide. There are abundant tilapia, channel catfish, puntat (Chinese catfish) and oscar throughout the islands as well.

Oahu Fishing Areas

The largest peacock fishery on the island of Oahu is the Wahiawa Public Fishing Area north of Pearl Harbor off the Kamehameha Highway in the central portion. The area includes a portion of the privately-owned Wahiawa Reservoir (commonly called Lake Wilson) and comprises approximately 300 acres of fishable water. While the family plays on Waikiki Beach, you can travel by car to the unique reservoir just 35 to 40 minutes away. I have fished Lake Wilson twice in the past 10 years or so and caught decent size fish both times.

The Wahiawa impoundment was constructed in 1908 by damming the deep gorges of two small mountain streams. Thus, headwaters exist on each end. Bordered by a few housing developments, an armed forces reservation, pineapple and sugar cane fields, and papaya and flower plantations, the V-shaped lake extends around the town of Wahiawa, running about a 15-mile course. Much of the property is privately owned and leased by a sugar company for their sugar plantation.

The long and narrow lake was dammed and dredged. If you include the military arm, the waters cover almost nine miles. The average depth of the 200 yard wide irrigation reservoir is about 65 feet!

Water clarity varies throughout the year. An algae bloom every once in a while turns the water a dark green. When the water level is stable and high, though, the lake is relatively clear. When it rains, the runoff from the mountains darkens it, and when the water level drops 10 feet, the lake also gets a little muddy.

The lake's water level may fluctuate 30 feet during the course of a year's drawdown (for irrigation). A relatively high water level puts water up into the trees and bushes that are abundant along Lake Wilson's shore. A falling water level won't affect the fish much, but rising levels turn off the fish. Tremendous deep-water structure exists due to the sharp slope of the lake's banks, and that is often where peacock bass are taken. The shallows are very limited on Wilson, and the presence of deep water nearby is common.

Wahiawa's North and South Forks

Peacock bass congregate in a couple of coves at the entrance to the North Fork of Lake Wilson. The fish are usually in huge schools that move in to cooler water. At certain times of the year, the water temperature can be from 5 to 7 degrees cooler near the rocks at the mouth. You'll also find a few smallmouth bass on the rocks.

The South Fork of the lake also holds peacocks all the way to the outfall. In fact, the outfall was one of the most popular peacock bass hotspots. The population of peacock have dwindled over the years, according to locals. Poachers have taken their toll, especially when water levels are low and the peacocks are spawning. The criminals take more than their limit and they take the spawners out of season.

When the water temperature reaches the high 70s, a pair of peacocks will get together and pick a spot along the Lake Wilson bank to spawn. They'll guard that nest once the eggs are laid, and they won't leave it. Anglers and poachers can get very close to the fish at this time. From the time they select a spawning spot, to the time that the eggs hatch into small fry, adults will be together.

The spawners are normally not feeding at all, but a lot of the poachers will drop a jig or live minnow on the bed. They'll agitate the fish with repeated casts until it strikes the bothersome bait with a vengeance. That's when the peacock will get hooked. The poachers will usually catch both fish off the nest, according to local guides. Thus, the fry's rate of survival is very low, and over the years, the peacock population has been affected.

The prime months for peacocks are May, June and July during their major spawning period. Bill McMeechan and a friend once caught and released 15 peacock bass weighing from 3/4 to 2 pounds and another 7 which ranged from 4 to 6 pounds one sunny day. The former Oahu resident is the first to admit that the action is not like that every day. That was an exceptional catch.

The Wilson schooling tucs normally range from under a pound to 1 1/2 pounds. If you can get a lure under the schools without getting hit, you should be able to catch the larger fish which are usually underneath. Often the peacocks will feed for an hour or so in the early mornings and late afternoons. The lake's peacocks are so aggressive at times, the smaller ones will chase the lure all the way back to the boat. If you have a fish on, there may be a dozen others trying to take the lure away. You may frequently have multiple hookups.

Wilson Facilities and Regs

Wilson's waters are usually a greenish tint and many anglers there opt for line with minimum underwater visibility. Berkley's ultra-low visibility green Trilene XL is a favorite of many for its close match to the reservoir's water.

The sharp slope of the lake's banks offers excellent deep-water structure, and that is where most of the peacock bass can be found.

Wahiawa State Freshwater Park is located along the South Fork of the Reservoir (southeast end of the lake) and includes a boat launching ramp and vehicle-trailer parking areas. When the reservoir falls 25 feet, as it does during extreme droughts, the boat ramp is not usable. Most of the boats on the lake are either homemade or inflatable. Some are "belly boats" or innertubes whose "captains" use swim fins to maneuver. Rental boats are seldom available, however, the Hawaii Freshwater Fishing Association (HFFA) is usually willing to aid visiting anglers in lining up a guide on any Hawaiian waters.

Currently, a freshwater game fishing license (a 30-day tourist license can be obtained at most sporting goods) and entry permit are required, and all persons must possess a readily-available life saving device, even when fishing from shore. Regulations at the time of this writing require that from February 1 through March 31, all largemouth (and smallmouth) bass measuring over 15 inches must be released. From May 1 through July 31 (spawning months) all tucunare (peacock bass) over 15 inches must be released. The bag limits at the area are 3 bass and 4 tucunare. Check with local officials for current laws, closed seasons and special regulations such as a maximum size limit before you plan your trip.

There are other fishing areas in the islands. Most reservoirs, stream banks and even stream beds in Hawaii are privately owned, however. Unless the waters are officially designated as Public Fishing Areas, fishing is allowed only by special permission from the landowner. Fishing is allowed in most State Forest Reserve Areas.

Kauai Fishing Areas

Kauai, the "Garden Island" offers the most and best peacock action, if you can access it. The beautiful island has more than 150 reservoirs (lakes and ponds) that range in size from two acres up to the 1,000-acre Waita Reservoir. For good peacock action and a chance at a bonus largemouth of 8 or 9 pounds, try the Puu Ka Ele Reservoir.

Virtually all of Kauai's impoundments are privately owned and were constructed as irrigation reservoirs for pineapple and sugar cane fields. Some plantations will issue permits for fishing in their lakes, which contain excellent populations of peacock bass. I've fished several of the small ponds and lakes on Kauai, and all seem to have excellent numbers of largemouth and/or peacock bass. You won't beg for action here.

Probably the best way to access a variety of waters is to hire a guide. It is among the best deals you'll find on the relatively expensive island. Several have gained exclusive access to private impoundments. I fished some of the lakes with a resident of Kauai who had access permission. A few guides who reportedly specialize in catch-and-release fishing for peacocks are Tom Christy (PO Box 1371, Koloa, Kauai, HI 96756; phone 808-332-9707), Phil Torian (P.O. Box 3525, Lihue, HI 96766; phone 808-822-1405), and Jack Gushiken (P.O. Box 151, Kilauea, HI 96754; phone 808-828-1041).

Several small reservoirs west of Koloa offer daily action of up to 20 peacocks per person when the timing is right. Most of these peacock bass will be in the two- to three-pound class. While the average size peacock provides plenty of action, an occasional tucunare up to 5 or 6 pounds may increase the adrenalin. Largemouth of eight pounds and smallmouth up to five pounds are also taken from some of these waters each year.

The peacocks in the reservoirs on Kauai's North Shore are a little fatter, and the scenery is more spectacular. The waters on this island, particularly along the North Shore, are deserted most of the time. Locals are seldom interested in freshwater fishing.

Virtually all of Kauai's impoundments are privately owned, however, some plantations will issue permits for fishing in their lakes, which contain excellent populations of peacock bass.

Two of the most productive peacock waters on Kauai are Tanaka Pond (located just 10 minutes from Lihue Town) and Slogetts (located on the mountain side of Kapaa Town). Neither allow boats, for liability reasons. Access to them can be obtained by writing to Lihue Sugar Plantation Co. Ltd., 2970 Kele St., Lihue, Kauai, HI 96766. To access the excellent peacock fishing in Waita, you can obtain a permit from Industrial Relations Manager, McBryde Sugar Co. Ltd., Eleele, Kauai, HI 96705.

Topwater Timing

Fishing for peacocks is productive all year, but April through August is the best time for topwater action. During the winter, rains are more frequent, but anglers still catch peacocks. It can rain for several days at a time in the winter, so be prepared if you travel then.

Spawning in Hawaii waters can occur from March through October when temperatures are around 80 degrees. Eggs are laid on rocks or other shallow hard objects and guarded by one or both parents; hatching takes place within four days, and parents guard the young until they are about three inches long. At least one parent is essential for survival of young, so fishermen are urged not to disturb spawning fish which are often visible near shore.

Hawaiian Tactics

When fishing for the small to mid-size peacocks of Hawaii, you can use the same lures and equipment that you do for largemouth bass. Schools of two- to three-pound peacocks can often be seen cruising the shoreline. School fish are very aggressive and competitive. They will hit just about anything, and several from the same school can often be caught.

You can sometimes see the fish in shallow or especially clear waters holding on the bottom or on structure. In fact, they can be stalked in the quiet coves of Hawaii's plantation irrigation ponds. Peacocks can often be sighted by rocks or brush which may offer a bedding site. The fish are very territorial and protect their nest and eggs, as well as guard their ''home'' habitat (even when no nest exists). When bedding, they will not move far.

Crankbaits, leadhead jigs, plastic grubs and floating minnow lures are productive on Hawaii's peacocks. Retrieve the lures in short, rapid jerks around a bed to draw a strike. Like a bedding largemouth, spawning peacocks will chase away annoying fish from their nest. At times, they seem to ''blow'' a small fish (and your lure) away rather than actually bite it. Once the peacock is irritated, it will generally take the bait into its mouth and carry it away from the bed. If you do catch one off a bed, quickly release it so that it can resume its mission.

Deep running cranks are a favorite of many for brushing off the points. They often kick up the silt on the Wilson bottom and attract some big fish.

Fly fishing around the schools of tilapia can be productive. The ''tucs'' like flies and small surface poppers. Spin and plug-casters toss small topwater plugs and buzzbaits for exciting surface action in the summer.

Live Bait Options

The most effective live baits are mosquitofish, mollies and small tilapia which are in most Hawaii waters. Threadfin shad are also very abundant in Lake Wilson. Anglers here often use free-swimming tilapia on a 1/0 hook. Even a dying bait can produce when cast to prime spots and slowly retrieved in a twitch-pause-twitch fashion back to the boat. After a dozen casts or so, an irritated peacock may put a stop to the nonsense and blast the tilapia.

It is not unusual to see a massive school of tilapia fingerlings swimming along in the shallows of a pond. All of a sudden, they become skittish and dart toward even shallower water as an ominous yellowish and olive "lightning bolt" explodes. Pods of disarranged tilapia are further scattered as the peacocks target the weak and injured. The water turns frothy as the efficient predators surge through the dismembered school of fish.

Catfish are very much in demand by peacocks as forage. Puntat, or "armored" catfish were introduced and peacocks readily feed on them. The peacocks reportedly go right in the catfish holes to catch one. The puntat is actually an air-breathing Chinese catfish that is a relative of the infamous walking catfish currently 'foot-loose' in Florida. The preferred bait size is four to five inches long, and some anglers net their own and store the hardy fish in holding ponds until needed for the hook.

Anglers will typically anchor several yards off shore and over a point that extends to deep water. They will thread their live baitfish on a No. 2 hook through its lips, toss it toward a point or stream bed intersection, and let it settle into 12 to 15 feet of water. After a minute or two, the productive anglers will move the bait a foot or two.

Contact Points

The Hawaii Freshwater Fishing Association, chartered in 1971, is a good source of fishing information. The association, which promotes freshwater fishing on the islands, can be contacted at Box 964, Wahiawa, HI 96786. It also promotes conservation and clean waters. Many of the HFFA are military personnel stationed at Pearl, Schofield, Wheeler Air Force Base or one of the other U.S. military installations on Oahu.

About 90 members of the HFFA are involved in fund raisers and efforts to keep Lake Wilson clean. They educate the general public on catch and release, size limits, spawning seasons, and negative impact of dumping exotic aquarium species into the lake.

Accommodations on these islands are relatively expensive, normally between $100 and $200 per night. That won't be a surprise to most. One I can recommend is the Hawaii Prince Hotel, (100 Holomoana Street, Honolulu, HA 96815; phone 808-956-1111) which is the newest hotel in the heart of Waikiki overlooking the Ala Wai Marina.

Other information on the island's freshwater fishing can be obtained from Hawaii Fish and Game Division, 1151 Punchbowl St.,

Honolulu, HI 96813; phone 808-548-4002. Tourism information is available from Hawaii Visitors Bureau, 2270 Kalakaua Ave., Suite 804, Honolulu, HI 96815. You won't need a foreign language course here, but two interesting words should pop up. "Aloha" means hello and goodbye, and "mahalo" means thank you.

Regardless of whether you spend your time on some of the beautiful Kauai irrigation lakes or on Oahu's Lake Wilson, you won't forget your peacock trip to paradise...unless you forget to take along the tackle!

Chapter 10

FACTS & FLOPS

Studies in Puerto Rico and Texas

Both Puerto Rico and Texas have done extensive research on the peacock bass. Puerto Rico's fishery is thriving, while the one in Texas has again met failure. To date, Texas' programmed introductions into heated power plant waters have not proved successful. Fish kills resulting from electric generators being shut down and waters cooling below the lethal limit have put Texas peacock bass experimentation on the back burner for the third time.

The research on the peacock by the respective fishery agencies in both places over several years has resulted in some interesting findings. Let's take a look at some of the facts confirmed or discovered by biologists in the state of Texas and the U.S. Commonwealth of Puerto Rico.

Puerto Rico's La Plata Reservoir

While peacock and largemouth bass evolved on separate continents (South America and North America, respectively), they co-exist in Puerto Rican reservoirs. Much of the Commonwealth's research on peacocks has been conducted on Puerto Rico's La Plata Reservoir. Largemouth bass (45 percent) dominate the impoundment's fishery, according to electrofishing results. They are followed by tilapia with 28 percent, threadfin shad with 12 percent, sunfish with 11 percent and other species, including peacock bass comprising about 3 percent.

While indications suggest that largemouth are much more abundant than peacock in La Plata, the latter are notoriously resistant to electrofishing. It is generally noted that the peacock abundance has been severely underestimated in the electrofishing samplings. In a 1989 gillnet study, biologists estimated peacock bass' relative abundance in the reservoir at approximately 12.5 percent.

Runoff from agriculture and cattle ranching is an important source of nutrient input to the reservoir. Correspondingly, excesses are responsible for occasional low dissolved oxygen levels and excessive growth of water lettuce and water hyacinth. The two floating plants occasionally cover up to one-third of the reservoir surface.

One of the most knowledgeable peacock bass researchers is Dr. Craig Lilyestrom, Peacock Project Leader for the Puerto Rico Dept. of Natural Resources, Marine Resources Division (P.O. Box 5887, Puerta de Tierra, P.R. 00906). His studies on the two freshwater, nest-building sportfish of similar size and body form have resulted in valid information on forage competition, reproduction and survival.

Forage Competition

One study looked at peacock and largemouth bass forage preferences and competition for food and/or space. Would competition be sufficient to limit numbers or size of one species or the other?

The study found that threadfin shad and tilapia fingerlings were the most important dietary items to peacock bass in Puerto Rico. Threadfin shad comprised 29 percent of all items consumed by number and 43 percent by volume. Of all stomachs with food, 50 percent contained threadfin shad. Tilapia fingerlings and fry combined accounted for about 3/4 of all food items. In a similar Hawaiian study, the most important peacock dietary items were tilapia, fish remains and threadfin.

In La Plata Reservoir, 15 percent of the peacock bass with food in their stomachs contained largemouth fingerling remains. Three percent of the largemouth stomachs examined contained largemouth fingerlings. By contrast, predation of peacock bass on largemouth was found to be practically non-existent in Hawaii. Since largemouth fingerlings were extremely abundant in La Plata, the opportunistic predators simply took advantage of it.

In Hawaii, studies showed the foraging relationship between the two species as "complementary in nature rather than competitive, given an adequate forage base." Peacocks and largemouth there are generally non-competitive in food habits. Hawaiian peacocks seem to favor shad and Gambusia minnows, while largemouth opt for

tilapia, according to fishery studies. Crayfish are a major component of the largemouth diet, but not for peacocks.

In Puerto Rico, the La Plata studies found minimal differentiation between the peacock and largemouth, probably because of the low diversity of forage species in the reservoir. The same reasons also account for the relative frequency of largemouth cannibalism and predation by peacocks on largemouth fingerlings. In La Plata, both species feed primarily on shad and tilapia. Crayfish are not yet present in Puerto Rican reservoirs, though they are sold in pet stores. La Plata largemouth occasionally include freshwater prawns in their diet.

Caribbean Spawning Studies

Mature peacocks were successfully captured at La Plata and spawned several times in 1991/1992 in ponds and tanks at a private tropical fish farm in Sabana Grande. After experimentation with aquarium-rearing techniques resulted in a successful spawn, a variety of fry-rearing techniques were tried. In the first attempts, survival of the fry in aquariums to "swimup" stage was generally low. When water temperature in rearing aquariums was raised to 84 degrees F., survival improved dramatically.

Spawning data generated from Lilyestrom's 1992 studies at La Plata revealed the major spawning periods of largemouth and peacock to nearly coincide, both peaking around February and March. The seasonal pattern of peacock bass maturation at La Plata seems to contrast with the peak spawning period of peacock bass in Hawaii, which is May-June. The latter months correspond to the normal rainy-season spawning period in the peacocks' native northern South America range.

Spawning of peacocks appears even more effective at another fishery project at Curias Reservoir, according to Puerto Rico biologists.

Island Environmental Factors

A water quality parameters study conducted in 1992 found that peacock bass seem to be more sensitive to high turbidity (suspended sediments) and low temperature than largemouth, but they are more tolerant of low dissolved oxygen than largemouth.

A large fish kill occurred in La Plata in December, 1991, due to low dissolved oxygen. A major flood on January 6, 1992 improved dissolved oxygen conditions throughout the reservoir, increased turbidity for several months, and removed nearly all floating aquatic vegetation. Water temperatures were severely and suddenly lowered by the flood, and only in May did they reach the level (about 84 degrees F) apparently required for successful rearing of peacock bass eggs and fry.

Throughout most of the study period, dissolved oxygen levels in La Plata were within an acceptable range, but with the major fish kill in December, surface dissolved oxygen levels dropped substantially in much of the lower half of the reservoir. The decrease coincided with the declining water temperatures and a period of high winds, causing a possible overturn of the water column.

Approximately 3,000 largemouth were killed, along with many threadfin shad, but no peacock were noted among the dead. The

January flood effectively reversed the reservoir conditions that were causing the fish kill, raising dissolved oxygen levels in the entire reservoir.

While the Puerto Rico study indicates that decreasing dissolved oxygen levels are more of a problem to largemouth, Florida experiences may reveal otherwise. In Florida canals, Commission Project Leader Paul Shafland suspects that low night-time dissolved oxygen can cause some mortality of peacock. He has noted that possibly peacocks are unable to move from areas with low oxygen levels at night when they become very inactive.

Sportfishermen reported capturing very few peacock bass while turbidity was high, whereas largemouth bass capture was considered normal. It may be, according to Lilyestrom, that peacock bass are less able to visually detect prey in turbid waters than are largemouth bass.

Texas Introductions In Heated Waters

In 1973, the Texas Parks and Wildlife Department (TPWD) began evaluating use of peacock bass in man-made lakes with heated waters from electrical generating plants. The power-plant reservoirs within the state presented new management problems; water temperatures were sometimes higher than preferred limits for largemouth and rough fish often became excessively abundant. Thus, cooling reservoirs were thought to be prime candidates for introduction of the predatory peacock.

The TPWD experimented with two species of peacock bass: the butterfly peacock and the speckled pavon. Biologists studied the species at their Heart of the Hills Research Station in Ingram, Texas. They also stocked fry or juvenile butterfly peacocks in five reservoirs in Texas. Peacocks were introduced only to power plant lakes with hot water discharges so that winter water temperatures would remain high enough for survival of the fish.

In 1978 and 1979, 3,753 peacocks were stocked in Bastrop Reservoir in Bastrop County. Coleto Creek Reservoir in Goliad County received 4,147 a year later, however, those two initial attempts to establish the peacock bass failed. The first winter after stockings were made in Bastrop and Coleto Creek, the power plants on those lakes shut down during a slack period in power demand. That allowed their waters to cool to a degree lethal to the peacock.

TPWD biologists decided to continue the program then, but at a very low level. The factors that led to that decision were the emergence in the state of coal-powered plants, which tend to be more

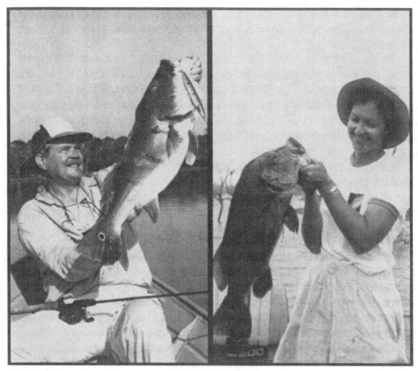

These are what Texas may be missing!

stable that those dependent on gas or oil. Because they are cheaper to operate, biologists believed that the coal-powered plants would be more likely to not shut down during slack periods in power demand.

In September of 1982, peacock bass were stocked in the public fishing waters of Tradinghouse Creek Reservoir in McLennan County near Waco. This 2,000-acre power plant reservoir received 1,600 peacock fingerlings. Alcoa Reservoir in Milam County received 6,456 in 1983-84. Many peacocks survived the initial experimental stocking and several reproduced for a brief period.

A Fishable Population at Wilkes

Much of their initial success occurred at Wilkes Reservoir near Marshall in Marion County. The Southwestern Electric Power Company's small reservoir in the northeast corner of the state, received 4,646 two- to three-inch fingerlings in September of 1981.

Many of those peacock bass grew to over two pounds in the 650 acre impoundment. About 20 six- to eight-pound brooders were also stocked, and for a while, fishing on the private lake was excellent. Wilkes was chosen for the experimental stocking of the two peacock species because of the control factor. The TPWD could better evaluate the impact of the peacock on the native bass and sunfish population without having to worry about fishermen catching them and carrying them off to stock in another lake. The studies on Wilkes found the peacocks to be prolific breeders, and an exceptional spawn occurred at the reservoir.

In the early 80's, the only fishable population of peacock bass in the continental United States was found at Wilkes Reservoir, but only the employees of the electric company could fish it. One employee caught two of the original brood stock, a nine pounder and an 11 pounder. If legally caught from public waters, the latter would have been a U.S. record for the species.

When Hot Is "Not" In The Lone Star State

Periodic power plant shutdowns on these warm-water impoundments resulted in massive winter kills and brought the program to a big halt. It appears that all peacocks ultimately succumbed to temperature extremes. Temperature tolerance studies indicated a lower lethal temperature of about 60 degrees F. and an upper lethal temperature of 102 degrees F. In most instances, cold winter temperatures were likely responsible for the demise of peacocks in Texas, but in at least one case, hot summer temperatures over 100 degrees F. eradicated a reservoir population.

From their initial studies, TPWD biologists concluded that the intolerance of peacock bass to low water temperatures appeared an insurmountable problem prohibiting any widespread use of these fish in the Lone Star state.

Research on, and freshwater stocking of, peacocks was discontinued in 1986, according to Dr. Gary Garrett of the TPWD. None have been taken in TPWD sampling or reported by anglers in several years. Today, peacock cichlids are believed to no longer exist in any water in Texas.

Despite that, the potential for the peacock bass in Texas should be enhanced by a trend toward multiple-unit power plants on some reservoirs. With such, it is unlikely that all units would ever be shut down at the same time. Thus, temperatures in those power plant lakes would be maintained at a level sufficient to insure peacock bass survival. Also, there's the possibility that peacocks could adapt to a slightly cooler water temperature and more fluctuation, once they are established in the cooling reservoirs.

Texas has an abundance of power plant lakes, and most should be capable of providing survivable water temperatures for the peacock. It also has some over-abundant forage problems. The peacock is a predator that can control the rapid expansion of tilapia in warm waters of the state. It could also prove valuable in controlling bluegill populations.

The peacock seems made to order for the power generation reservoirs in Texas and other southern states. According to Dr. Garret of the TPWD, the state has no plans to work further with the peacock bass, and that's a shame!

Chapter 11

TOP TACTICS FOR TROPHIES

Trolling, school activating and other productive methods

The best areas in the lagoons of South America generally won't have freshwater porpoises. It seems that the bigger fish will be in the middle of the lagoons when porpoises are not present. Otherwise, the big peacocks will hide under cover along the bank

The best way to determine whether or not porpoises are in a lagoon is to inspect the shallow inflow from the river. If it is too shallow, they won't be in the lagoon. A porpoise won't go into an area where he thinks there's a possibility he may get trapped. Thus, a small ditch-type opening going into a lagoon (where perhaps you have to pull the boat across a sandbar to access it) is ideal. Chances are the porpoises won't be in that area.

If the lagoon is large, the best means to locate the peacocks is by trolling. Once you've found them, others should be in the same area. You can stop and cast and catch plenty of big fish. By trolling, you can cover much more water.

The big fish in the pecking order always get their choice of habitat. The little fish have to get out of the way. As a result, you won't generally catch little fish alongside of big fish. In most cases, the trophy-size peacocks want to be out in relatively deep water, in a bottom trench in a lagoon.

In waters relatively free of cover, such as the lagoons of Venezuela and Colombia, it seems that the top water action is more consistent. The lagoons and lakes in Brazil generally have a lot more cover in the form of standing timber, and they are slightly deeper than those to the

*S*andy saddles with shallow water dropoffs are productive spots for trophy-sized peacocks.

north. They really look more like little reservoirs although they are natural lakes off the river. There are numerous features like points and humps in Brazil lakes, and that's different from the majority of lagoons that you'll see in the Orinoco area of Venezuela.

Typical Haunts

In most peacock waters, you will find a few typical locations where peacocks hang out. Points are normally productive on all peacock waters. Cuts into the lakes and into the river from lakes are likewise productive.

A third situation could be the best spot in a lake: a saddle between two islands (like I found on Guri once) or between an island and a point. The sandy saddle I found on the Trombetas watershed in Brazil was approximately one-and-a-half to two feet deep. It had an extreme dropoff on one side, a fairly good dropoff on the other side, and there were several big fish on the deeper side.

Productivity Variables

Most shallow areas have some vegetation, and such spots may hold a few smaller peacocks. The best areas, though, usually have a relationship to deeper water; the thickest bush or tree in a bunch is often the best spot; two growing close to each other is often good; an

Casting to the deep water off a rocky point that drops quickly is a productive method.

isolated bigger tree or bush away from a group also has a lot of potential, especially if it lies near deeper water. The edge of the woods; timber around a depression, and the edges of fairly large openings in thick wooded areas also can be very productive.

As elsewhere, water conditions are critical when fishing peacocks. Both clarity and water level affect these fish. In most South American tributaries, waters are clear and dark. Turbid water which flows into an area as levels rise may cause peacocks to actively feed.

The other significant variable affecting tactics in South America is the water level and how fast it is rising. Regardless of color, high water makes catching peacocks more difficult. With the jungles beside lagoons flooded, fish are widely dispersed. Getting to them and keeping them out of entanglements can be very difficult.

Top Submergent and Surface Methods

Several methods can be very effective on most waters. Tossing or trolling Rat-L Traps is highly productive. Casting them to the deep water off a shallow point or ''saddle'' that drops quickly can be very productive. In Brazil, I caught three peacocks in about 10 casts with a Super Trap using this ploy. I was wading in calf-deep water and reeling the vibrating plug from about 14 feet of depth to about five just in front of me to generate the strikes. The fish weighed about 40 pound in aggregate.

Waters without the benefit of a sharp drop or other defining structure that are over six feet deep, should generally be trolled.

Waters of less depth and more large obstacles (whether boulders or submerged trees) should be cast. The new one and a half ounce Super Trap has proven to be one of the most effective big fish catchers of the submerged lures.

A second effective submergent producer is the minnow bait, particularly those seven inches long with saltwater hooks. Rebel, Norman, Bagley, several other companies make them. Such lures are primarily effective in waters three to eight feet deep, and will catch their share of big peacocks.

Spoons also can be deadly on giant peacocks, and trolling them is usually the preferred method. A heavy, single-hook version is ideal to attract the peacock. An extra large Tony Accetta Pet Spoon has accounted for a lot of giant peacocks in South America. A magnum casting Krocodile spoon is ideal for checking out heavy cover.

Perhaps the best lures for peacock bass are topwater plugs, specifically those with tail spinners. My favorites are the Big Game Woodchopper and the Magnum Jerk'n Sam. Two surface plug patterns are effective: cast and twitch the baits and troll the baits. On my last two trips, the latter was most effective. I had fished Venezuela's Lake Guri three times before learning about the trolling pattern while in Brazil. My partner and I employed it on the next to the last day of our trip.

Speed Trolling

We wound up trolling the topwater lures in a "speed-troll" pattern. We placed our eight-inch Woodchoppers with tailspinners only (I eliminate the front spinner) and huge Jerk'n Sams with tailspinners behind the boat and twitched them to kick up water as we trolled. Every second, we'd twitch it forward, let it pause it; twitch it forward, pause it; twitch it forward, pause it.

Many of the big fish would come up and explode on the baits, and this was something really unique to experience. If the big peacock missed the lure, he would come right back after it. He would hit it again if you didn't jerk the plug away so far that he couldn't relocate it. A few of the huge fish were briefly hooked and got off and then struck again. They finally got the lure and, after a good hook set, were eventually landed. All the big fish were released alive and well.

The top-water trolling method is ideal for calling up big peacocks from the middle of the South American lagoons.

There are usually more there than at the edge. Often, the big fish in a lagoon seem to be out in a deep slot, or anything that resembles

T op-water trolling is ideal for calling up big peacocks in South American lagoons.

a channel. In trolling, you're looking for a school, and specifically one of the school that will give himself away by striking the trolled lure. Just troll along at a pretty good speed and keep jerking the topwater lure.

Texan T.O. McLean believes that the bigger fish are caught trolling. The evidence that I've accumulated so far verifies the same. McLean has taken peacock up to 22 pounds with the technique. (His largest peacock, a 24-pounder, was caught casting a 7-inch Rebel.) I have caught (and witnessed my partner catch) dozens of peacocks over 15 pounds that were taken while trolling.

School Activations

Peacocks readily school in most waters they are in. That's one of the reasons they are a great fish. Schoolers can be seen occasionally on the surface in the larger lagoons of South America and in Guri Lake. The majority of time, however, they school below the surface. Most of the school will be comparable in size: five-pounders generally run with five-pounders, and 15-pounders hang out with 15-pounders.

*O*n more than one
occasion, my
fishing partner and I
have caught doubles.
Most of the school will
be comparable in size.

Often, a couple of good anglers can catch four or five peacocks from the same school before the feeding frenzy subsides. Some of the action may go on for 15 minutes, or 30 seconds. You can motor to the boiling activity and then drift with the school in order to have several shots at them. Action with packs of roaming peacock is fast-paced.

On several occasions my partner and I have caught doubles. We'd hook a big fish, stop the boat to play it, and the other person would cast in the general direction of the strike. That would result in another strike from an equally large peacock bass. And we're talking fish of 12 to 16 pounds in general.

On one occasion, a 13-pounder was taken right at the boat on a cast lure. On another occasion, my partner was fighting a four-pound peacock, leading him toward the boat when another peacock, much larger, grabbed the four-pound peacock and took off. He fought the fish for about 10 or 15 seconds before the little peacock popped out of the mouth of the huge one.

He reeled in the little peacock which was all cut up. That smaller peacock was totally inside the mouth of the big peacock. Unfortunately, the lure inside the mouth of the little peacock did not get its trebles into the bigger fish.

N etting a double catch of trophy peacocks weighing 39 pounds is impressive anywhere!

More Giant Doubles

On another occasion, we had a double on, apparently our largest of the Brazil trip. One of the fish had enough power to pull off drag at a tremendous clip and straighten a 60-pound Cross Lok swivel. The other fish also pulled off a lot of line and broke 30-pound test line. There were no frays in the line. It had just been checked prior to putting the topwater bait out into the area. Both of those fish had to be 20 pounds or more. The area certainly offered such.

On many occasions, my partner and I were able to work our trolling pass with the big topwater baits to locate a peacock, stop the boat while catching one, and cast the area to catch one or two more. In many cases, the partner would catch a second fish. The first fish would be unhooked and that person would catch his second fish casting the same area. On several occasions a trolled bait simply left out behind the boat and twitched (after a strike on the other bait) would generate a second strike!

My most memorable catch using this technique just happened to be the largest pair of peacock bass ever landed at one time, that I have seen or heard of. Dick Ballard and I were trolling a productive stretch of water in a small lagoon of no more than 15 acres. We had caught a couple of 15- to 17-pound peacocks in two previous passes.

On this short pass along relatively open water, a monster exploded on Ballard's large topwater bait, and the guide quickly shut down the motor. I continued working my big surface plug toward the boat as my partner struggled with his giant peacock. As soon as the bait reached the boat, I fired another cast to the general vicinity of the first strike and began my jerk-jerk-pause retrieve.

On the fourth jerk, you guessed it, another monster pavon exploded on my bait. We both had the brutes on, and the bell for the "battle royale" rang. We had to maneuver past each other, rod-over/rod-under, a couple of times during the fight. Both fish neared the boat at the same time and our guide adeptly netted the two giants.

Ballard's fish weighed 19 pounds and mine 20 pounds on the certified scales we had brought along for my record chase. The double weighing 39 pounds was most impressive!

One tactic that may seem crazy to some is used by some guides on Lake Guri and other places in South America. While drifting along a row of trees or along the shoreline, they will occasionally splash the water with a paddle. The noise seems to attract peacocks that believe others in their clan are feeding on the surface.

Minnow-Bait Comeback

Another tactic that seems very effective is in response to a topwater strike that misses the mark. Throwing the same lure right back in on top of the fish may score, but tossing a long minnow plug and slowly (quietly) reeling it past the fish usually triggers the strike better. You and your partner can team up with this tactic, and you should certainly have a second rod rigged for employing the "minnow-bait comeback."

Simply leave the topwater bait at the scene of the swirl and quickly fire the minnow bait to the spot, if you are the only one in the boat fishing that territory. Or your partner can be ready for such a miss and quickly toss to the boil when it happens. This is similar to a "tease operation" described in my chapter on fly fishing peacocks.

When you get the peacock to the boat, often you find others in the school trying to get at your lure (in the hooked fish's mouth). Cast another lure to that spot and you may very easily have more action from a free-swimmer.

Chapter 12

TACKLE FOR THE FRESHWATER BULLY

Here are the keys to productive lure selection

Choosing the best peacock lures normally depends on establishing effective patterns for the size of fish you are targeting. Just like when fishing for largemouth bass, prime locations and presentations are fairly easy to determine. So are the most productive lures.

Peacock bass readily strike most artificial lures, but can they do damage! The strikes are jolting, and the fish are tough on equipment. They can chew up lures to the point where they won't run straight. Peacocks can and do, pull stainless steel hooks out of lures, straighten 3X hooks, tear out screwed-in hook harnesses on wood lures and strip gears in inadequate reels. At other times, they will pull off line down to the bare spool.

Schooling peacocks are so aggressive that fishing a lure with more than one hook can lead to multiple hook-up excitement. In some schooling situations, the challenge is not in hooking a peacock but in landing it. If a fish misses the bait, another will blast it.

Here's another trick that you and an alert partner can utilize to catch more peacocks. Whoever is not fighting the fish should make a quick cast near the battling peacock, and often, he'll hook a second fish. Peacocks school, and members of that school will often follow a hooked fish right to the boat. The hangers-on will be after the bait or lure hanging from the unfortunate fish's jaw. It's a tactic I've used often, successfully.

There is absolutely no need to take light tackle. In fact, the best lures are those expressly designed for musky, stripers or saltwater

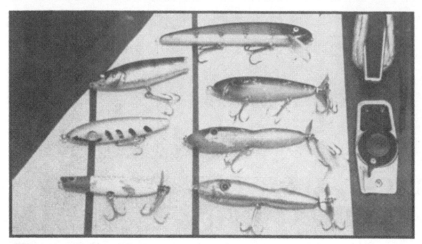

*P*eacock bass readily strike most artificial lures, but can they do damage!
The strikes are jolting, and the fish are tough on equipment. They can
chew up lures and pull the stainless steel hooks out, straighten 3X hooks, tear
out screwed-in hook harnesses on wood lures.

species like snook. I fish topwater baits about 80 percent of the time,
but under certain conditions, those lures that move in a deeper pattern
will produce better.

Multiple treble hooks on a plug are a good idea in general. They
can mean more fish. I and several of my avid peacock fishing friends
have caught two fish on the same plug. It is not unusual to have one
fish on each treble hook of a plug. The second fish apparently has
tried to take the plug away from the first ''unlucky'' peacock.

Topwater Plugs

I've found top surface lures for the giants to be Luhr-Jensen's Big
Game Woodchoppers and Jerkin' Sams (both 6 to 7 inches long).
These huge lures catch monster peacocks in Venezuela and Brazil,
rest assured. They are in their prime when cast toward shore, but they
are also highly productive fished in ''open'' water and when trolled!

Topwater prop baits (with one spinner on the rear) are often most
productive for giant peacock bass. Some of the giant baits, like the
Woodchopper, come with two (fore and aft), and I believe that you
stand a better chance of catching these fish without the front prop; the
action is better to attract peacocks. You won't have line abrasion
either from a front spinner if you simply take it off and screw the long
line tie eye back into the bait.

Huge surface lures catch monster peacocks in Venezuela and Brazil, whether cast toward shore, fished in "open" water or trolled!

I normally prefer a sharp jerk moving the bait approximately two feet, but sometimes a long hard pull is more effective. At other times, a soft twitch draws the explosive strike, particularly when near cover.

Fish the baits quickly toward wood cover; as you get close to the key habitat, slow down the plug and work it with a short rip, then pause, and rip it once again. You want to keep the lure in the prime attraction area as long as possible. Fish around the tree tops, over points and along channels or roadbeds (in a reservoir).

While cigar-type topwater plugs and other surface baits without props do attract peacocks, most of the time the fish are attracted more readily to the rear-spinner floating plug.

Minnow Plugs

Long minnow plugs that wobble down a few feet certainly catch their share of the fish. White and silver hues are generally most productive. I've found the Heddon RedFin to be very productive on the giants. Other good minnow baits are 6 to 8-inch long Magnum Rapalas, Bang-O Lures, Bomber Long A's, and similar plugs with appropriate hardware (see section later in this chapter for details). Top colors are gold, blue and white.

Long, shallow-running minnow plugs can be trolled slowly close to shore, typically in water 3 to 8 feet deep. They may pick up rotting leaves which cover the bottom certain times of the year, but that's all the more reason to employ plugs that float.

Working the minnow plugs by short rips is very effective. A fairly fast retrieve can also be hot, and as a follow-up bait, these lures have no peer.

Working the minnow plugs by short rips is very effective. A fairly fast retrieve can also be hot, and as a follow-up bait, these lures have no peer. When a big peacock boils at your topwater presentation, come back at it with a minnow bait slowly retrieved through the same spot. Hang onto your rod tight, though.

On Lake Guri in my ''formative'' years of peacock fishing, I and two fishing partners worked on a big fish for 30 minutes one time. We were in a flooded jungle cove and the monster had boiled on each of our topwater plugs several times without getting hooked. The strike was almost automatic; every seventh or eighth cast that fell on the spot generated the strike on the second or third twitch.

Finally, I picked up a 7-inch Rebel Minnow and waited for my two partners to move their baits clear of the spot. I then tossed my lure to the prime spot, twitched it once and started a very slow retrieve. The lure wobbled about three feet before the ''freight train'' hit. Back then, I was using only 25 pound test - what a mistake.

The fish went into submerged trees on each side of the boat, and I luckily work it free of the entanglements. Then, about the time I worked her to within 10 feet of the boat and away from the emergent tree cover, she got another head of steam and bulled straight down. I felt the tree limbs abrading the monofilament as it surged into

A *large selection of lures is necessary to be prepared for successful peacock action.*

never-never land. And that was it for me. We had several views of the peacock which probably weighed 18 pounds or more, but I never did get to take that picture.

Once you have an initial strike, that fish has given itself away, and it can be caught with a follow-up presentation. Under some conditions a following fish is more tempted by a slower follow-up presentation. Often, though, if you want the eyes of the peacock to glow red (a red slash may also appear under their gill plates) with excitement, a violent follow-up retrieve is best. The lure action will turn these fish on, so work the baits hard!

Searching The Depths

Best baits for submergent operation include jigs, spoons and vibrating baits that go into the depths to attract the fish. As a rule,

A vibrating plug can be deadly on giant peacocks when fished in water between visible cover.

use baits that weigh at least 3/4 of an ounce. I prefer those that weigh about twice that much.

Jigs And Vibrating Plugs

When fishing water between visible cover, a vibrating plug can be deadly on the giant peacocks. I have found the new 1 1/2-ounce Bill Lewis Super Trap to be the best. It has the weight to cast and stay deep and the appropriate hardware for the world's "baddest" bass. Good colors are silver with black or blue backs, yellow or gold, white and green.

You can dispel a myth that peacocks only feed near the surface by simply dropping a jig into the depths. One of the most deadly lures on peacocks is a one ounce white bucktail jig. When the cover allows their use, you can't go wrong with a heavy jig. While I typically search for giant fish attracted to topwater action, others may want to employ more of a "sure thing" in relatively unencumbered waters for numbers of peacock. Yellow jigs and those with a touch of red are also very productive.

Spoons And Spinners

The Luhr-Jensen #18 Tony Accetta Pet Spoon is very productive on big peacock bass. When the giants are not on the surface, trolling

The best rod should be blank-through construction and rated for heavy line and heavy lures. A powerful hook-set is a must!

one of these lures will draw the strikes. Most any large spoons with some shine and a single hook or giant treble will produce when trolled. A large Krocodile spoon in a bright orange color may also be effective.

Spinnerbaits can be effective on peacock bass (particularly in the hottest months on lakes and lagoons). My wife Lilliam caught her largest peacock ever, a 13 pounder, on a one-ounce "musky" spinnerbait. It was a windy day on Lake Guri, and the big topwater plugs just weren't fooling the fish. I had never seen a peacock caught on a spinnerbait, but that changed abruptly; her peacock was the largest taken on the lake that day.

Lilliam's lure was almost destroyed, however. Its stout wire arm was mangled, although the single 6/0 stainless steel hook (partially straightened) held. A spinnerbait will normally be wrecked after a peacock encounter, so take plenty along if you insist on tossing them

Attention to Detail

To catch big fish on large plugs, you must pay special attention to details. Each morning on the way to the fishing ground, my hooks are honed razor sharp. After each fish, I touch up the point also. Take a spare box of hooks along to change out those that aren't up to the task of surviving a peacock bass. It is frustrating to have a pile of lures at your feet with their hooks either mangled or missing! Lures with small, questionable-strength split rings get a second one added prior to the trip. In fact, double split rings on most all small baits are vital to landing the big boys. A peacock will open all but the strongest split rings. The double split rings may stiffen the hook harness somewhat, but it offers much added strength. Heavy-duty Berkley Cross-Lock swivels will provide additional security.

Appropriate Tackle

To tackle giant peacocks often around cover, you'll need heavy equipment, lines testing 30- to 40-pounds and stout medium-heavy action rods with either baitcasting or spinning gear. I normally have three or four rods rigged up while fishing. I prefer throwing heavy baits on a 7-foot Berkley Series One graphite rod matched with a Daiwa MagForce casting reel. I also employ a 6 1/2-foot medium heavy action Series One for lures weighing less than one ounce. When traveling to South America, I'll usually take along five rods and five reels, although I only take three in the boat. Redundancy is paramount when you're a long way from the nearest tackle store.

The rod should be blank-through construction and rated for heavy line and heavy lures. A pistol grip handle won't provide adequate hook-setting power. A long handle behind the reel allows you additional leverage during the battle with these tough-fighting fish without interfering with accurate casting.

Spool the reel with 40 pound test Big Game line, or try some of the new 45-pound test braided line. You need a line with low stretch and good abrasion strength when fishing around wood cover. Trophy-size peacocks will often break 25 pound test line like sewing thread, so take along a bulk spool if you insist on using line of less strength. If your quarry is a giant payara, then you may also want to use a heavy, 40-pound test wire leader.

Peacocks are sometimes hard to hook because they have a tendency to bite down on a lure. Thus, a powerful hook-set is a must to have the hook penetrate the fish' mouth. Make sure the reel you use has a smooth drag system. You'll need it.

Bring enough tackle because giant peacocks will try to destroy what you are offering them. There's an evening ritual that occurs around most sport fishermen in South America; it's called sitting around the table straightening and replacing bent hooks, re-rigging tackle, etc. recounting the ferocity of the day's quarry.

Chapter 13

FLYFISHING EXCITEMENT

Peacocks love to feed on the surface

Peacock bass are perfect flyrod fish because of their proclivity toward surface feeding. Their fondness for feeding in the shallows make popping bug manufacturers happy.

An eight- or nine-weight outfit which will handle poppers in the 1/0 class is ideal for most situations, but you can go lighter or heavier. When fishing larger flies for the giants in South America, you'll appreciate the heavier rod.

In the Amazon jungle of Venezuela and Brazil, you should be proficient in handling heavyweight saltwater-sized tackle and have the stamina to cast big flies and poppers for long periods in a hot sun. When after giant peacocks, those of 15 pounds or more, experienced fly fishermen may opt for a 10 or 11 weight rod and saltwater tapers.

Fly Class Records

The fish in South America are big; in fact, three fly rod tippet world record applications were approved by IGFA for fish taken just two weeks prior to my first venture to Pasimoni. Fort Walton Beach angler Bert Bookout, who holds a couple of fly class records, caught a 25-pound, 8-ounce peacock on 20-pound (10 kg) tippet, 8-weight 8 1/2-foot flyrod and large saltwater popping bug. The fish that taped 39 1/2 inches long and 24 inches in girth, was just one pound off the all-tackle world mark!

Bookout's friend, Al (Elverton) Clark, caught a 19-pound peacock the same week on 16 pound tippet for an IGFA record. Clark caught his fish on a home-tied, heavy-duty popping bug. Clark also caught a short-lived IGFA 20 pound tippet record weighing 13 1/2 pounds just two weeks earlier while fishing on the Cinaruco River in Venezuela.

Bookout's fish, which was released back into the same waters, is the largest caught on the Pasimoni River. In 1992, the big fish from that watershed was taken by woman angler Ami Nash of Birmingham. It was certified by IGFA as a 20-pound line class world record. I'm betting that several of the next flyfishing world records will come from this area.

Wading Action

Many of the river networks off the huge Amazon and Orinoco Rivers offer hard, white sand bottoms, with numerous sandbars and points that seem to concentrate the peacocks. Such places, particularly those in the smaller tributaries, are prime spots for a fly fisherman to wade.

On good days, you can fool 10 to 20 fish along the shallows of most lagoons and lakes in South America. A fly fisherman wading off the points will catch plenty of small fish to keep things interesting and will occasionally attract a large peacock or other giant on the right fare. As you might expect, the average size fish caught on flies while fishing from river sandbars in South America is usually considerably smaller than those caught on the giant topwater baits by plug casters fishing in the lagoons.

While wading the hard, sandy bottoms, your only concern should be stepping on a freshwater stingray. I saw several in the Rio Trombetas area of Brazil. There's really no cause to be worried about the piranha, unless you are bleeding.

Streamers And Poppers

An angler shouldn't be content to fish a single fly pattern in any peacock waters. Take along a wide assortment of flies and the loudest poppers you can find.

Standard streamers and bass bugs tied on Number 2 or 1 hooks are often consistent producers of small to mid-size peacocks in canals, lagoons, ponds and even South American rivers around sandbars. An assortment of big poppers and extra-long streamers tied on 1/0 and 2/0 hooks are ideal for mid-size to large peacocks in the same areas.

For large to giant peacocks, Stu Apte tarpon flies, Deceivers, Seaducers and Dahlburg Divers (hair bug) tied on 2/0 to 4/0 hooks are productive patterns. Larger, bulky saltwater patterns like Lefty's Deceiver (an effective all-around streamer), Kime's Saltwater Fly

A fly fisherman wading off the points will catch plenty of small fish to keep things interesting and will occasionally attract a large peacock or other giant on the right fare.

(white body with red hackles) and durable Fender Flies also fool the huge peacocks of South America.

Large popping bugs that ride high in the water and make a loud splash, rather than a "pop", are most effective. You want the bug to toss water off as it moves forward through the potential strike zone. For the peacock's attention, it is best to jerk a lot of noise and water action.

Streamers of three to five inches long on a heavy hook will enable you to get the fly quickly to any fish feeding on the surface. Another option is to use lead wrapping to sink the fly quickly.

Colors and Patterns

Expert fly fishermen recommend a Hare's Ear Nymph, a Silver Doctor, and the famous Royal Coachman dry fly. A sinking Clouser minnow streamer with lead barbell eyes is a favorite of some peacock chasers who wish to explore slightly deeper waters. Both silvery and colorful imitations with mylar glitter strips and bucktail attract the active peacocks. A strip of white rabbit fur with its icing of tinsel can be productive.

When the peacocks are on the bed, some fly casters toss a bright red or orange streamer to cruise through the nest. Some of the most productive streamers are standard steelhead or salmon patterns like the Skykomish Sunrise, Thor and Sabine.

While color combinations have minimal impact on the number of strikes, the most effective fly colors for peacocks seem to be green/white, olive/white, blue/white and chartreuse/white and the optimum lengths in South America are 4 to 6 inches or more.

A small No. 4 epoxy Muddler Minnow fished against a canal bank in South Florida or in Lake Gatun in Panama is often productive. Weighted marabou streamers work equally well, but as with any streamer, you may miss some scary explosions on top.

For the small butterfly peacocks of Panama, a friend recently used a two-material fly tied on a 1/0 340011 Mustad hook. Called ''Pfeiffer's Delight'', the body was bump tinsel and the wing (front and rear) and tail was created with a touch of glitz tassel material. The silvery fly closely resembled the small sardine minnows that were so abundant in Lake Gatun.

An Ethafoam popper and 3/8-inch live-body closed cell popper with saddle hackle tail and ice chenille collar, both tied on 1/0 hooks, were also employed to catch the aggressive fish.

Cast-and-Retrieve Tactics

In most slow-moving or current-free waters, fly fishermen will do well to cast toward the bank from the boat. The closer one can cast to shore consistently, the better the chance of catching big numbers of peacocks. The smaller ones in particular spend much of the day lying in the shallows where schools of forage fish may swim by.

The most effective retrieve for streamers is to exercise 12-inch strips, pausing to allow the fly to breathe. In large waters with ''grande'' peacocks, a slow presentation is ideal, while in more confined waterways full of small, aggressive fish, the faster retrieve is usually very productive.

One trick that enhances the opportunities is throwing small rocks into the area you are fishing. The commotion will draw evil-tempered peacocks from 30 to 50 yards away to see if their compadres are feasting on a wayward school of baitfish. Then, you simply have to put a fly to the fish.

Another way to use the flyrod effectively without blind casting unproductively for an hour or so is to have a partner tease them up

L *arge popping bugs that ride high in the water and make a loud splash are most effective to attract the peacock's attention.*

with a hook-less propeller plug. Once the aggressive fish are excited, tossing a quieter popper or streamer will often result in a hookup.

Many successful fly fishermen prefer to follow someone who is plugging with a large surface lure. The plug creates enough disturbance to attract interest from nearby peacocks. But, once in a while, the peacock may refuse the huge topwater offering and a fly follow-up is the right choice.

Outfitting For Location

Some anglers may use a light trout outfit, such as a five-weight, and flick pencil poppers along shallow shoreline structures to catch small to mid-size fish. Heavier gear is usually required in most areas, particularly those in South America. Virtually all of the peacocks, which grow to giant proportions in the Amazon and Orinoco watersheds, are catchable on fly tackle, though. Some tackle requires more effort (and expertise) than others.

The fly angler visiting South America will need to bring, as a minimum, a 9- or 10-weight rod with both weight-forward floating lines and sinking tips of various densities. He'll appreciate a 9-foot long, 10-weight fly rod to handle explosive giants.

Another productive flyfishing method is to have a partner tease up the peacocks with a hookless propeller plug. Once the aggressive fish are excited, tossing a quieter popper or streamer often results in a hookup.

A four-piece rod and cloth carry-on case can easily fit in the plane's overhead bins. Billy Pate, Abel and Sage reels with strong drags and large line capacities can be loaded with weight-forward floating, sinking and sink-tip lines. Another carry-on can hold flies, leaders and tools.

Leader and Tippet Thoughts

The abrasiveness of a peacock bass' jaw is slightly worse than that of a largemouth, so careful anglers will frequently check for abrasion. Shock leaders are not necessary, but some fly casters will employ a 30-pound shock tippet which is adequate for most peacock action. A loop knot is often used with heavy monofilament for attaching the flies.

If you are fishing river areas, you may want to take along some wire leader material for piranhas and other toothsome species. You will lose some tackle when fishing South American peacocks. These fish are big and strong.

Fly fishing the small irrigation impoundments in Hawaii is a rapidly growing sport. Hawaiian anglers normally cast surface

In smaller ponds and canals, flies are often the bait of choice and may catch more fish than plugs and jigs. At times, peacock bass are not picky about colors or patterns.

poppers to the aggressive peacocks which are found under the abundant tilapia at times. When located, the peacocks readily strike flies, as well as the small poppers. Bluegill and smallmouth bass are also caught with fly tackle, as are rainbows on the island of Kauai. Some of the fly fishermen on that island also are guides who specialize in peacock fishing trips.

Rod Weights

Fly fishermen in Hawaii catch smaller fish on number seven fly rods with small, flashy streamers tied on number four hooks. While most hooked on a fly rod are less than four pounds, some anglers have caught peacocks weighing up to eight pounds, six ounces on as little as two-pound tippets.

Casting in shallow waters along deep drop-offs using quick, short strips is usually productive. The key to fly fishing peacocks in most places is persistence. Often, if you can see a fish, you can catch it. However, you may have to make 30 or 40 casts before it will take the fly.

A seven- or eight-weight graphite rod is ideal for the peacocks in Florida, Puerto Rico, Hawaii and Panama. Drop the fly near an underwater snag and let it settle. When it is seven or eight feet deep, began twitching it back towards the boat, pond or canal bank. Along the canals of Dade County, toss the fly to a likely spot at the foot at a cattail clump shaded by one of the numerous Brazilian pepper trees.

Stripping School

In smaller ponds and canals, flies are often the bait of choice and may catch more fish than plugs and jigs. In fact, at times, peacock bass are not picky about colors or patterns. Slow, water-logged retrieves will often fool the fish, as will fast surface strips.

Most small water peacocks in locations outside of South America prefer to slug it out in open water rather than retreat for cover along a sharp drop of the bank. That fact further negates the need for heavy gear.

In South America, you can often cast to numerous schools of fish and catch a seemingly-endless variety of species. Flies will also attract the fly-slashing Sardinata and other jungle species in Venezuela rivers. The Sardinata is a schooling fish that migrates into the shallows to feed. It is a silvery, tarpon-like fish with large diamond scale pattern and yellowish head and fins. They grow to about 10 pounds, but, like most of the species around the Equator, they fight much larger.

Chapter 14

BOAT-SIDE BATTLES

The world's most explosive freshwater fish

Just 15 feet from our boat, the bass exploded on my surface plug showering the emergent trees in three directions. I reared back on my stout seven-foot rod to set the hooks as the giant swirled on top of the five foot deep water. The big fish felt the 3X extra-strength hooks, dove toward the bottom, and then headed skyward.

This huge bass wasn't a largemouth, but a 16-pound peacock bass that wanted to tear up anything in its way. My guide gasped, "Grande pavon," as the sight of the peacock's broad triple-striped side caused my partner's mouth and eyes to open wide. I was too excited to blink. It swam toward the boat and under it as I reeled frantically to keep a tight line.

I thrust the rod toward the brushy bottom, praying that this giant would not become entangled or straighten my heavy-duty hooks harnessed on the Jerkin' Sam topwater expressly for the Venezuela trip. I ran forward on the bow deck with rod tip well below the water's surface to keep pressure on the big fish. I was confident the 30 pound test line wouldn't part, unless it was grated against some of the flooded hardwoods that surrounded the boat.

The peacock exploded on the opposite side of the boat just a few feet off the gunwale, as I worked the rod's tip below the trolling motor and brought it up once again to fighting position. I pressured the bass, but it didn't respond; it headed into the top of a flooded tree off the stern of our boat. Steady pressure on the fish for about 30 seconds worked her free and out of that entanglement.

My guide, Juan, did everything he could to make sure my trip was successful, even jumping in and diving for the fish.

I again put some pressure on the brute, but it was heading pretty much where she wanted. She bulled past my guide's outreached net and into another tree top at the bow of the boat. She became entangled there and shortly swam out...the same way she swam in. The monster again swam into a brush top off our stern, and this time steady pressure didn't work her free.

We waited for a good two minutes for the peacock to swim out of the tree and to the surface and Juan's net. Finally, Juan decided time was running out and stripped to his underwear. Everyone should have a conscientious guide willing to swim beside the boat with giant peacocks. Right?

Guide Overboard Maneuvers

This was about the fourth time that Juan had jumped overboard, albeit to retrieve hung up lures in the other cases. I was not surprised by his action and was thankful of his willingness to go hand to hand with my trophy fish. I'm not sure if he thought about the two super

B oat-side battles are plentiful on Lake Guri in Venezuela.

strong trebles on the plug hanging out the jaw of the still-powerful peacock. He simply jumped in and dove straight down for the fish. My steady pressure on the fish all of a sudden made her move. She shot out of the tree top, toward my diving guide and the boat. I held my breath as she passed Juan without one of the hooks making contact with his sun-wrinkled hide. When the huge head of my peacock erupted from the surface beside me, I jabbed my hand toward its jaws. I guess that I wasn't thinking of the lure's dangerous adornment at that instance.

I put a lip lock on the fish and hauled her over the side. Juan's head bobbed to the surface in time to see my capture, and his grin confirmed his satisfaction with the events, despite his ''bath'' in the middle of my action with the ''grande pavon.'' My partner, Berkley Bedell, congratulated me on my success with the big fish. He had given me encouragement throughout the battle, and now it was time for some photos.

This boat-side battle took place in the flooded jungles of Venezuela's Lake Guri, the second largest impoundment in the world. We were a short distance from the beautiful Guri Lodge near the hydroelectric dam facility. We were in a wooded arm off the main

A trophy-size peacock is almost impossible to control. It takes to the air several times with gill covers rattling as it tries to throw the bait.

lake that we named "Monkey Cove" after the howling monkeys that yelled back and forth across the cove.

Dumb, Mean and Powerful

In several trips to the jungles of Venezuela and my more limited exposure to the hard-fighting peacocks in the South Florida canals, I've come to the conclusion that a giant peacock is not very smart. They are just mean and powerful. A largemouth has a purpose in heading into heavy cover when hooked, and that is to break the line in the entanglement.

A giant peacock will head into brush or a tree top because it is there. The peacock doesn't have a strategy in mind, like tying a knot around the limb. It is big enough to do what it wants and go where it wants to. The peacock is like the proverbial bull in a china closet. He doesn't pay attention to the small stuff.

Contact and Initial Run

A trophy-size peacock is often impossible to stop on its initial run. Once it feels too much pressure on the line, it takes to the air several times with gill covers rattling as it tries to throw the bait, or it turns and heads toward the boat. Then as though getting a second breath of air, a giant will again take off away from the boat. Having the expertise to adjust the reel's drag and a great deal of luck comes into play then.

On many occasions, I had 9- to 12-pound peacock bass go into submerged trees and with steady pressure was able to lead the big fish back out the way it had entered the brush. Seldom have I been able to do that with a giant largemouth bass that is seemingly buried in an entanglement. The largemouth generally knows not to come back out the way it went in.

Fight To Exhaustion

The peacock just won't give up, until it is exhausted. It has a much stronger burst of energy than a largemouth or smallmouth, yet once that energy is depleted, the fish is over-stressed and may die soon if not cared for properly. The black bass family is more hardy than the peacock, and once you get a lip lock on the largemouth or smallmouth they are relatively docile due to being partially paralyzed by the hold. That's not so with a peacock - a lip lock is just a way to grab them; they probably think that they have a good bite on your hand.

When a giant peacock bass is hooked, you won't want to play the fish long underneath the boat or near either the outboard or the electric motor. If the fish makes a run, the best move is to point the rod into the water beside the boat and swing it around the end (bow or stern) of the boat.

When a fish is active at boat-side, there are few fishing thrills more memorable. Different species behave differently, and larger ones all put up a good fight, but the peacock bass is the best fighter of all. The battle grounds of excitement for most of us is right at the gunwale. It's a place where the smart angler will usually win!

Chapter 15

BIOLOGY AND LIFESTYLE

Behaviors are becoming to this brute

Peacock bass are substrate spawners capable of reproducing more than once per year. In most tropical areas, some peacocks can be found breeding each month of the year. The masses, however, will usually breed once or twice a year. This is often just before and during the rainy season in areas that have such, according to biologists reports.

Sexual Maturity

According to some fishery research, given sufficient food, young butterfly peacocks grow to sexually mature sizes between 11 and 13 inches in less than 12 months, while the speckled peacock take three years to become sexually mature. According to other fishery research, females of both common species mature at about the same rate. In many South American rivers, peacocks reproduce once a year; in reservoirs, they may spawn three times a year.

Pre-Spawn Behavior

The sexually ripe male is normally identified by a pronounced forehead "hump" of fatty tissue that is stimulated by sexual maturity. Recent scientific evidence also exists that some females may exhibit a small "hump" as well. The hump is reabsorbed within several weeks after spawning. The male will cruise an area for up to several days while searching for "display grounds." A prominent courting location near a suitable spawning site is selected to present himself to females that pass by. He will aggressively defend his territory from other males.

When a female stops, the male will intensify lateral displays and begin digging a bed area. The female will leave and return to the spot several times before the pair will bond and the male (who is generally much larger than the female) will lead the female to a specific nesting area. Once the pair has bonded, spawning will occur in about two weeks.

After bonding, both fish will help dig one or more shallow beds for newly hatched larvae. They will also clear an area for egg deposit near the depression beds. Any external disturbance (predator) coming toward the nest areas will cause both fish to quickly depart.

The size and depth of the depression bed varies depending on type of bottom material. In soft clay or sand, the shallow depression may average six inches in depth and 18 inches in diameter. The depth of such beds will vary due to the water clarity and other predatory factors present, but the sides are steep which helps to contain the larvae once they are deposited. The natural depressions in fallen trees, stumps and other firm submerged objects often serve as nest areas for deeper spawning peacock bass.

Spawning Behavior

Spawning normally takes place on a flat surface that has been cleared (or is bare to begin with) of algae or other debris during the fanning movements of the parents. This could be on the top of a stump or the bark of a fallen tree that lies horizontal below the surface, yet near to the depression beds. The female moves over the bed and deposits neat rows of eggs as the male follows and exudes sperm which drifts down over each row. This effort usually takes several hours. Reports state that peacocks may lay an average from 3,000 to 10,000 eggs, with an average being about 5,000.

The color of the eggs reportedly change from a white to a yellow as they develop. Underdeveloped eggs accumulate a fungus and are normally removed from the bed by the parents. Ultimately, less than one percent of the eggs will hatch and reach adulthood. The eggs, while being constantly fanned by the female, develop into larvae in about two days.

Some males periodically take part in the fanning to remove foreign materials from the eggs, but their time is often consumed by defending against egg predators. From time to time, the male will leave the female to fend off a threatening intruder. By the time the eggs hatch, the female exhibits very aggressive behavior toward any intrusion, while the male offers aggressive lateral displays and circles the area.

T he sexually ripe male is normally identified by a pronounced forehead "hump" of fatty tissue that is stimulated by sexual maturity.

Post-Spawn Behavior

As the eggs hatch at the spawning site, the male (and sometimes the female) takes them into his mouth and deposits the fry in the nearby small depression beds. The larvae have a mucous-like adhesive at their head which allows them to stick to the bottom of the nest. They wiggle their tails, making the floor of the bed resemble a writhing mass of undulating worms.

At night, the parents lower themselves over the bed to discourage nocturnal predators from attacking the larvae. Both parents stand vigil and guard the brood which mill about their nest deriving nutrition from the remnants of their yolk sacs.

As the fry become free-swimming, which occurs about three days after the hatch, the parents herd them around the canal. The fry stick together in a cloud near the surface of the water. They feed throughout the day on zooplankton, growing rapidly and becoming stronger.

Shared Parental Care

The parents guard the young for extended periods of time, sometimes up to 10 weeks, and that assures a continuing population for years. The parents chase off any would-be predators, but when they are guarding the fry, one may instantly intercept any lure in the

*T*he average size of most peacock bass is around 3 or 4 pounds, but in many South American waters, several between 6 and 10 pounds may be taken on a good day and in a few select places, monsters over 15 pounds are caught occasionally.

neighborhood with a terrifying rush. Although not feeding during this period, this defensive action makes the fish susceptible to some fishing pressure.

"It is not unusual to see two adult peacock bass and maybe 1,000 young swimming along with them in the South Florida canals," notes biologist Paul Shafland. "Once the fingerlings are three inches long, they usually separate. One day I noticed two peacocks, each about three to four pounds, swimming with a cloud of young. I cast a small jig into the cloud and caught one of the fingerlings. It was five inches long and still being guarded by its parents."

Juvenile Growth

When the small fry reach an advance fingerling stage, they are on their own. They move into shallow cover and fend for themselves. Biologists describe color pattern changes occurring then from a lateral stripe to the three vertical bars. Fry will go after insects and tiny freshwater shrimp, where available, for their food source.

The fry will remain in the shallow cover for about five to six months before moving into more open-water habitat. Their diet will change to include more small, shallow-swimming minnows. The fingerlings form schools and become very aggressive while foraging. The most mature, usually a male with pronounced hump, and most aggressive fingerling will generally be the leader of the school.

The butterfly peacock bass grow about an inch a month during the first year of life, so they are 12 inches long in just one year. Like many other cichlids, male peacock bass grow faster and larger than females. Biologists have reported that the maximum growth of female butterfly peacocks is approximately half the size of the largest males.

Adult Growth

Growth of butterfly and royal peacock bass continues to be rapid to sizes of 2 to 3 pounds after which it may slow. The speckled peacock has reportedly a fairly uniform, continuous growth rate until it dies of old age. The average size of most peacock bass is around 3 or 4 pounds, but in many South American waters, several between 6 and 10 pounds may be taken on a good day and in a few select places, monsters over 15 pounds can be caught occasionally.

The most common and widespread peacock species, the butterfly peacock attains a smaller maximum size of 11 to 20 pounds, than does the speckled peacock, which is 27 to 32 pounds, depending on which fishery biologist report you happen to be reading. In Venezuela, the weight of the butterfly peacock is greater in reservoirs, up to 12 pounds, than in their natural river habitat, which is never larger than 9.5 pounds.

Puerto Rican biologists did a length-weight relation analysis of largemouth bass and peacock bass less than 17 inches in length. They found that the largemouth are slightly heavier than the peacock at comparable lengths. In comparing similar studies in Hawaii, the biologists concluded that both sexes of peacock bass in their primary fishery at La Plata Reservoir were slower growers. The Puerto Rico peacocks were found to be of relatively lower weight at any given size than either their male or female Hawaiian counterparts.

Following are length and girth measurements, in addition to weights of large peacocks that I and my boat partners have caught and released in South American waters. Most of the weights were calibrated on 3 different scales, one of which was certified for accuracy according to world record-keeping authorities.

DATA COLLECTED IN THE AMAZON

I used the information to develop a formula by which one might estimate the weight of a fish simply by taking its measurements. We are all familiar with the standard formula for largemouth bass which is Weight = length x girth squared / 800, or W=lxgxg/800. For peacock bass, I propose the following formula: Wt. = lxgxg/750

	WT.	LGT.	GIRTH		WT.	LGT.	GIRTH
Casiquiare	22	37	26	Brazil	17 1/2	32	20.5
Peacocks	22	37	23	Peacocks	16 1/2	32	20
	20	36	22		16 1/2	32	19
	20	33	23		16	30	–
	19	35.5	22		15 1/2	30.5	18
	19	35	22		15 1/2	31	19.5
	18 3/4	34	22		15 1/2	32	19
	18	33.5	20		15	30	19
	17 1/4	34	20.5		15	30	19
	17	33	20.5		14 1/4	30	18
	16 3/4	33	20		14	30	17
	16 1/2	32	20		14	30	19
	16 1/4	32	20		14	30.5	--
	16	32	20		13 1/2	30.5	18
	15 1/2	31	19.5		12 3/4	30.5	–
	15 1/4	33	19.5		12	27	17
	15	32	18				
	14 1/2	30	20	Lake Guri	13	28	18
	13 1/2	29.5	18.5	Peacocks	12	27	17
	13 1/4	32	19		9	25	--
	12 1/2	30	18				
	12 1/2	29	19				
	12 1/4	29.5	18				
	12	29	18.5				
	9	28	16.5				
	7 3/4	27	15.25				

Note 1: For an obviously spawning female, add 5% to the Wt. value.
Note 2: For peacocks under 25 inches use Wt. = lxgxg/850.

Foraging Preferences

While it has been reported in some magazines that the peacock has the "unusual characteristic of changing seasonally from vegetarian to carnivore," no scientific evidence exists that supports the claim. That, I'm afraid, is just another of the numerous falsehoods and misconceptions that have been published in magazine articles and books regarding the peacock bass. According to the fishery studies that I've researched, adult peacocks feed exclusively on small fish,

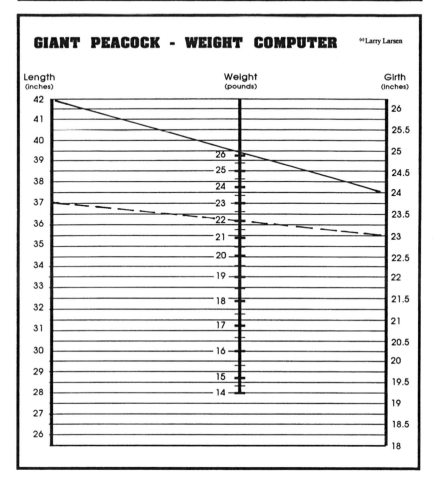

GIANT PEACOCK - WEIGHT COMPUTER (c) Larry Larsen

especially on threadfin shad, mosquito fish, tilapia and bluegill in U.S. waters.

In stomach content analysis of peacocks in Lake Guri, Venezuela, Corporacion Venezolana de Guayana (CVG) biologists found larger peacocks exhibit extensive cannibalism over smaller peacock bass. The speckled peacocks studied were also found to have ten different types of food grouped in four fish families. The butterfly peacocks in the study were found to have six different types of food grouped in three fish families.

In a Hawaiian study, absence of largemouth bass in the stomachs of 591 peacock bass suggests they do not prey significantly on largemouth. Peacock bass in South Florida canals have been found to feed on tilapia and other exotic species, rather than the less abundant native forage species.

In Florida waters, butterfly peacock communities have been able to control undesirable exotic fishes. Such results demonstrate introductions of peacocks can be an effective fisheries management tool. Forage fish in the canal system in Dade and Broward Counties average 13 pounds for every one pound of predator fish. Classically, fisheries biologists normally consider three to six pounds of forage to one pound of predator as being ideal, according to Shafland.

"What makes the peacock right for that habitat is their ability to harvest the over-abundant spotted tilapia," he explains. "The peacock is an opportunistic fish that will eat what's available, and that's mostly the spotted tilapia. A four-pound peacock may represent 30 to 40 pounds of the forage fish that its eaten. This allows us to convert a very abundant and under-utilized resource, the spotted tilapia, into a very highly utilizable sport fish, the peacock bass."

Bass Feeding Comparisons

There are distinct differences between peacock bass and largemouth bass feeding behavior, according to Shafland. For example:

1. Peacock bass appear to be more mobile than largemouth bass, primarily using their great speed to run down forage rather than relying on ambush tactics.

2. Unlike largemouth bass, peacock bass feed only during daylight hours with peak feeding occurring in the morning. This strict daytime feeding pattern is to be expected since peacock bass become inactive at night, as are most other cichlids.

3. Peacock bass tend to feed in shallower water often at the shoreline's edge or nearer the surface when in deeper water than is characteristic of largemouth bass. For these and other reasons, adult peacock and largemouth bass are generally thought to be non-competitive predators.

4. Peacock bass tend to feed on forage fish that are about one-third of their length more often than do largemouth, and are more cannibalistic of young peacock bass as well.

P iranha often chew on the tails or fins of the hooked peacocks during the course of a battle.

Foreign Competition

There is competition in South America, however, and it can be tough! The bluegill-size red piranhas are to be feared, according to the local Indians. The black piranha which grows to six pounds, on the other hand, is not the schooler that swarms en masse over any "meat" that comes along. It is a carnivorous fish, however, with typical piranha teeth.

Piranha often chew on the tails or other fins of the hooked peacocks during the course of a battle (or before). I've seen piranha bite the belly of a big peacock as we fought the fish. At times, a pack of piranha may go after the peacock, miss him, and bite through the line. Even when I didn't seem to catch piranha in some South American lagoons, I still found peacocks with fins that had been freshly snipped.

Small piranha don't generally hang around big peacocks, though. The peacocks feed on them. In the same respect, you likely will never catch a four-pound peacock around the giants.

Many South American waters also offer another interesting competitor for the forage, and that is the prehistoric-looking payara. The sport fish are numerous in swift-flowing rivers. In lakes, like Lake Guri, the fish seems to hang out in depths of 30 to 70 feet beside huge flooded trees near the submerged river channels. The silvery, fanged fish runs to 15 or 25 pounds and are the most unique catch in reservoirs.   When fishing for the saber-toothed fish there, wire leaders are almost a necessity.

Survival of The Fittest

Both the butterfly and speckled peacock have very little chance of dying if you simply catch them and release them right away. If you hold them out of the water for a long time, they can get stressed. They don't relax easily when out of the water like the largemouth. The thumb lock on their lower jaw won't temporarily immobilize them either. They will wiggle and bang until they regain their freedom.

The peacock is very temperature-dependent, and as a result is range limited. It dies at about 60 degrees. Fortunately, the water temperature in the South Florida canals seldom falls below 70 degrees, and the lowest recorded in the past nine years was 66 degrees. The box-cut canals which expose relatively small amounts of the water to colder air temperatures are responsible for the ideal over-wintering environment. Obviously, in Central America and the islands, the water temperatures are very conducive to the introduction of the fish.

Peacock bass prefer waters of relatively low pH (generally between 5.0 and 6.0). In waters of high sediments, they do poorly. In stained acidic waters below pH 6.5, they do well. In clear waters that are nutrient-poor, there are usually fewer peacocks and more species of other fish with which to compete.

Chapter 16

TRAVEL TIPS/REQUIREMENTS

Health, Timing, Equipment and Expectations

The travel agent or tour promoter has you booked for one of the great peacock trips to an exotic land. The guides and boats are arranged, and you have looked forward to the annual sojourn for months. Expectations are high, as they should be, but when you get there, some of what we avid anglers call the basics may not be present.

It doesn't matter whether you are going to a Venezuelan lake after giant pavon or to South Florida after some of their rapidly-growing butterfly peacocks. You need to be prepared. What you take along should be well thought out, in advance. What you can expect to find will facilitate better planning on your part.

Travel Requirements/Options

You will need a valid passport to enter Venezuela (and most countries that offer peacock bass fishing). A tourist card will normally be provided by the airline carrier for your flight to such a destination. These documents, along with your receipt for your payments of departure tax, must be presented to customs official when you leave the country.

Both a valid passport and visa are required to enter Brazil, and the latter takes a few weeks to obtain. Your visa is good for only 90 days from your date of departure. Check with your tour promoter well in advance for other travel requirements and restrictions to all destinations. When visiting a foreign country, try to travel during the weekdays for ease of enduring customs when reentering the U.S. Expect to pay a departure tax upon leaving most countries and even some cities within.

*W*hat you take on your overseas fishing trip should be well thought-out and planned to make your experience more enjoyable.

On most trips arranged by reputable overseas tour operators, an English-speaking ground services representative will meet you upon arrival in the destination country. A bilingual ''operations manager'' normally accompanies each group during all ground transfers. The flights on Varig, Viasa, and American Airlines to many of the peacock destinations are generally on comfortable wide-bodied aircraft. Most offer superb in-flight meals and good movies to wile away the 3 1/2 to 5 hour flight time.

Health Precautions

You should be in good health if you are traveling into the jungles of South America. You may be several hours from the nearest airstrip and several more hours from the nearest medical facility. Although malaria and yellow fever are not a problem in most areas, the U.S. Public Health Service recommends protection from these diseases for people traveling to some destinations in the Amazonas. Consult your physician about precautions such as malaria pills (larium tablets) and yellow fever immunization.

I feel that you should carefully watch what you eat and drink in all foreign destinations. Drink plenty of bottled water when you are fishing near the equator. Some well-traveled peacock explorers that I know bring beef sticks and canned lunch meats from home to ensure the ''quality'' of some meals.

C lothing for most of the fishing trips to peacock destinations should be light weight, light colored and comfortable in the to-be-expected heat and humidity.

Clothing and Personal Items

Clothing for most of the fishing trips to peacock destinations should be light weight, light colored and comfortable in the heat and humidity. The traveler to South America, in particular, will have to be prepared for the sun and air temperatures of 80 to 100 during the day. Most of the fishing locations are near or right on the equator where the sun tends to burn through sunscreen quickly.

Quality polarized sunglasses, long-sleeved cotton shirts, long pants and a wide-brimmed hat are wise to protect yourself from the sun (and bug bites). Some anglers also prefer the sun protection of a bandana covering their neck. Take sunscreen (SPF 22 or higher) for your exposed face, neck and hands. A plastic insulated ''sport bottle'' with plastic straw may aid your intake of cooling refreshments, if the camp operation offers only large bottles of soft drinks.

In some locations, you'll need a good insect repellent with at least 95 percent ''deet''. For no-see-ums, I have found Avon Skin-So-Soft to be excellent. Put your sunscreen on first and insect repellent on

*P*eacocks and rain go together, so never leave home without your lightweight rain gear.

last. To further protect your ankles in bug-infested areas, take along long socks. Surprisingly, you can wear shorts and short-sleeved shirts in some South American jungle areas without concern for bug bites. Your tour operator should be able to advise you on the specific destination.

You will want a few changes of clothes, but remember that in far away jungle destinations you will not be dressing up and dining out. Take a minimum of casual clothes along on peacock expeditions. The atmosphere at the lodges and camps is always informal. Some even offer a daily laundry service. For example, even when camped on the side of the Pasimoni River in Venezuela's Amazonas Region, I was able to leave dirty clothes behind each day for our cook/laundress to wash in the black-clear river waters and hang out to dry.

Never leave home without your lightweight rain gear. Peacocks and heat go together, and so do peacocks and rain. From Miami to Hawaii to Central and South America, the Tropics usually account for more rain than we normally get in places further north. A windbreaker may be comforting on some commercial flights and in the evenings

Some vital pieces of equipment in any peacock bass expedition include a scale and measuring tape.

at some destinations. Even in the jungle at first light, the breeze can be chilling. A waterproof gear bag is handy in the boat.

A small first aid kit should be taken on any peacock trip, because these fish may be out to get you. Also bring along any medication you may need, some aloe lotion for potential burns, and a "sting-ese" medicine for the obvious. Including a small flashlight (and batteries) in your travel pack is smart.

Packing Tips and Tricks

Pack all your gear in soft duffel bags, limiting it to 55 pounds, specially if you're traveling on small planes to very remote destinations. Always take a carry-on bag with essentials and a heavy-duty rod case. Try to put a couple of reels, lures, camera and film in your carry-on bag, if possible, in case some of your luggage gets lost.

Your name and address should be permanently marked on each piece of luggage. Check your own luggage at the ticket counter and carefully count each item each time you transfer by plane or van. Don't let someone else handle your claim tickets, but do have the baggage handler keep your bags together. Personally watch them being loaded into bus, van or taxi.

Your rods (be sure to include a few extras) should be well protected in the rod case. I wrap soft clothing around the tips and the bundle of rods before sliding them into the case. Extremely long, one-piece rods may not fit in some small charter planes.

Timing Your Venture

The best fishing months in peacock destinations vary widely, even among tributaries a few hundred miles apart. The worst times are those near or in the rainy season, and most peacock destinations have one. High water disperses the fish over a huge area and back into vegetation, trees and bushes. They can be very difficult to locate under such circumstances. Some rainy seasons last four months while others may take up six or seven months. Afterwards, it may take up to two months before some areas offer good fishing again. Find out when the dry season falls and schedule your trip for a date then. Failure to know such can result in below-par fishing trips.

The Right Equipment For Handling Peacocks

Several things are vital to any peacock bass expedition. They are: a pair of long-nose pliers, a knife (Old Timers are great ones), a pair of light-colored gloves or a thumb guard (glove), a scale and measuring tape (both Berkley and Stren make good lightweight 50-pound scales), and a lip-lock grabber (Tempress makes a good one which has a pliers-type arrangement with a little nail in it that secures the lower jaw of the fish once you get it in his mouth).

Normally your guide will handle all fish for you. Typically, he will use either a large, long-handled net or the squeeze-action fish jaw grabber. An alternative method is the tail grab and lift. You'll need the lip-lock or a glove to hold up a giant peacock for photos. Don't try it without one or the other, or your fingers can quickly be turned into hamburger over the course of a day.

Pliers are necessary to get the hooks free from the fish; with the size of some of the peacocks being caught, there's no way you would want to get a hook out without pliers. A knife is sometimes needed to cut out a hook from the toughest part of the peacock's mouth.

A lip-lock grabber to hold up a giant peacock, and pliers, are a necessity in most peacock waters.

The Right Mount

Once you catch the monster peacock of your dreams, you'll need to measure the length and girth and take a few good color photos for the taxidermist to work from. One who specializes in peacock bass is Don Frank, Don's Studio Taxidermy, 7812 Westridge, Raytown, MO 64138 or phone (816) 356-1990. He does a great job!

Don has been a full time taxidermist since 1980. He has mounted thousands of fish and has won over 60 state, national and world taxidermy competition ribbons. Don is also known for the woodcarvings of world record size fish that he is doing for Bass Pro Shops in Springfield, MO. The taxidermist has been to Venezuela twice to fish for peacock bass and to collect fish to mold for fiberglass reproductions.

Catch and release is becoming popular because of the difficulty in transporting fish through airports, customs and layovers. By releasing the giant peacock bass, the fishery can be maintained for years.

Don presently has a variety of molds available for peacocks weighing up to 22 pounds. With peacocks, a fiberglass replica is by far the most practical, thus the importance of the measurements and photo. Skin mounts of peacocks reportedly do not last near as long as those of largemouth bass or other common North American species.

Other Fishing Tackle You'll Need

You'll need a hook file or hone to keep the hooks as sharp as possible and line clippers. The good tour operators offer a list of effective lures and tackle that you'll need to be productive on their particular trip. One mistake that too many traveling anglers make, and I've seen it a few times with people from some tour operations, is bringing along tackle that is not adequate for the peacock bass.

Definitely, you'll need 25- to 30-pound test line and stout medium-heavy action rods on all South American jaunts. The fish there are big and strong. For focusing on peacocks between 15 and 25 pounds, I normally prefer 40 pound test Big Game monofilament when not specifically addressing line class record setting.

Any quality baitcasting reel should be able to handle a peacock, and if you're an experienced fisherman, the smaller baitcasting reels are the way to go. They are more lightweight and will contribute less to fatigue in the long hours of fishing with, often, giant lures.

You may want to carry along steel leaders for use around schools of piranhas in some South American waters, but I would not use them with heavy line when fishing for peacocks unless you experience a ''bite-off'' in a given area. Some waters are full of heavy timber and a tight drag is necessary. In others free of snags, setting a lighter drag is recommended. That will save some ''break-offs'' and may keep split rings and lure screws from failing (and save some lures).

The one thing you can count on regardless of your drag, line size or expertise is losing some tackle. Check out the chapter on tackle for details about lures and other fishing equipment.

Portable Electronics

In remote areas, such as the Amazon jungle, one piece of electronics that should be provided is a short-wave radio (unless phones are available). On large waters, like Lake Guri, when boats may go 15 miles away from the marina or launch, a CB is a valuable piece of equipment. Most of the better outfitters offer such.

PEACOCK TRIP CHECKLIST

☐ Tickets	☐ Flashlight (w/batteries)
☐ Passport, visa	☐ Heavy-duty rod case
☐ Tourist card	☐ Carry-on bag
☐ Tip money	☐ Camera, film
☐ Health precautions	☐ Rod, reels
☐ Medications, pills	☐ Appropriate tackle
☐ First aid kit	☐ Long-nose pliers
☐ Light weight clothing	☐ Knife, hook file
☐ Polarized sunglasses	☐ Gloves, thumb guard
☐ Long sleeve shirts	☐ Scale, measuring tape
☐ Long pants	☐ Lip-lock grabber
☐ Wide-brimmed hat	☐ Line clippers
☐ Sunscreen (SPF 22 or higher)	☐ Steel leaders
☐ Deet insect repellent	☐ Portable electronics
☐ Rain gear, windbreaker	☐ Spanish/English phrase book
☐ Waterproof Gear bag	or electronic translator

Anglers may want to take along some electronics of their own in some situations. While the well-equipped Ranger bass boats on Lake Guri, which stretches 80 miles in length and averages 22 miles in width, have sonar, most of the boats in foreign lands don't. Many fishermen, me included, appreciate the information that a good depth finder provides on unfamiliar waters. Catching more fish and having some feel for depth below the boat are heart-warming reasons.

South America is one of the sport fisherman's last frontiers. As such, the conveniences we take for granted, such as one or two sonar units and an electric trolling motor on every boat, are non-existent at most destinations. Guides may use a paddle or even the outboard motor to move around the flats and a fishing rod to check the depth. Carrying along a trolling motor and battery (and charger) is not realistic, but packing a portable sonar is.

Guides with just a couple of seasons of fishing experience generally don't have the knowledge of the avid weekend bass angler relative to the importance of a sonar unit. They know simply where fish have been caught in the past. On my first visit to Lake Guri (prior to delivery of the Rangers), I was fortunate enough to have brought down a portable sonar unit, portable power pack and transducer.

While you can modify a fixed unit to be portable (I did once using a lawn mower battery), it is much wiser to buy a portable LCG. When being transported, they should be in sturdy and lightweight cases with the face well-protected. When in use, they can usually be mounted right to the battery pack which keeps the unit more manageable in the boat. Most have convenient carrying handles for transporting.

Traveling with the go-anywhere units is easy. For the average stay of a week, you shouldn't even need a charger. One caveat though, is that if you are traveling to a foreign destination and will have to clear customs with a relatively new-looking unit, don't transport the unit in the original cardboard box. They may think you are carrying the unit to their country for resale.

Knowing when you will need to carry along the portable should be found out well ahead of the trip. Ask the tour promoter or boat rental agency about the sonar equipment aboard the boat you'll be fishing from, and get it in writing if possible, so that there will be less confusion at the fishing hole. If they have none, take your own.

The Guides, Language And Tipping

Most guides at peacock destinations are very accommodating and able to handle fish very well. Seldom will you have any problems with ineptitude while a fish is at boatside. Some may not know the water as well as you might believe, particularly if they are covering over a 100 miles of river and dozens of lagoons. I've seen situations where some guides did not remember certain ways in and out of very remote lakes. Some even frequently stopped to ask locals in dugouts about the better areas to fish.

The tour operator will generally suggest an average tip for the fishing guide, cook and camp staff. That total may average from $100.00 to $150.00 per fisherman, per week in South America. The local camp manager may suggest that this should be "pooled" for the whole staff, but you may want to tip your own fishing guide individually. Baggage handlers in the airports during ground transfers are normally tipped about 50 cents per bag in foreign peacock destinations.

While the camps in Spanish-speaking countries always have English-speaking people in camp, a Spanish/English phrase book or dictionary may come in handy for communications with some guides. Pocket-sized solar-powered electronic translators are available for around $25 to $30, and I can recommend a handy reference guide called "Spanish For The Fisherman". The booklet can be purchased for about $4.00 from Dick Stevens, 2719 So. Depew St., Denver, CO 80227 or phone 303-985-4957. The language aid is always worthwhile to bring along.

FISHING & HUNTING RESOURCE DIRECTORY

If you are interested in more productive fishing, hunting and diving trips, this information is for you!

Learn how to be more successful on your next outdoor venture from these secrets, tips and tactics. Larsen's Outdoor Publishing offers informational-type books that focus on how and where to catch the most popular sport fish, hunt the most popular game or travel to productive or exciting destinations.

The perfect-bound, soft-cover books include numerous illustrative graphics, line drawings, maps and photographs. Many of our **LIBRARIES** are nationwide in scope. Others cover the Gulf and Atlantic coasts from Florida to Texas to Maryland and some foreign waters. One **SERIES** focuses on the top lakes, rivers and creeks in the nation's most visited largemouth bass fishing state.

> ### THANKS!
> *"I appreciate the research you've done to enhance the sport for weekend anglers."*
> R. Willis, Jacksonville, FL

All series appeal to outdoors readers of all skill levels. Their unique four-color cover design, interior layout, quality, information content and economical price makes these books your best source of knowledge. Best of all, you will know how to be more successful in your outdoor endeavors!!

ON VIDEO!
Lowrance Electronics Presents
ADVANCED BASS FISHING TACTICS
with Larry Larsen

(V1) This 50-minute video is dedicated to serious anglers - those who are truly interested in learning more about the sport and in catching more and larger bass each trip. Part I details how to catch more bass from aquatic vegetaion; Part II covers tips to most effectively fish docks & piers; Part III involves trolling strategies for bigger fish, and Part IV outlines using electronics to locate bass in deep waters. Don't miss this informative and entertaining opportunity where Larry shares his knowledge and expertise!

Great Tips and Tactics For The Outdoorsmen of the Nineties!

BASS SERIES LIBRARY
by Larry Larsen

(BSL1) FOLLOW THE FORAGE - BASS/PREY RELATIONSHIP - Learn how to determine dominant forage in a body of water and catch more bass!

(BSL2) VOL. 2 BETTER BASS ANGLING TECHNIQUES - Learn why one lure or bait is more successful than others and how to use each lure under varying conditions.

(BSL3) BASS PRO STRATEGIES - Professional fishermen know how changes in pH, water level, temperature and color affect bass fishing, and they know how to adapt to weather and topographical variations. Learn from their experience.

(BSL4) BASS LURES - TRICKS & TECHNIQUES - When bass become accustomed to the same artificials and presentations seen over and over again, they become harder to catch. You will learn how to modify your lures and rigs and how to develop new presentation and retrieve methods to spark the interest of largemouth!

(BSL5) SHALLOW WATER BASS - Bass spend 90% of their time in waters less than 15 feet deep. Learn productive new tactics that you can apply in marshes, estuaries, reservoirs, lakes, creeks and small ponds, and you'll triple your results!

> ### HAVE THEM ALL!
> *"Larry, I'm ordering one book to give a friend for his birthday and your two new ones. I have all the BASS SERIES LIBRARY except one, otherwise I would have ordered an autographed set. I have followed your writings for years and consider them the best of the best!"*
> J. Vinson, Cataula, GA

(BSL6) BASS FISHING FACTS - Learn why and how bass behave during pre- and post-spawn, how they utilize their senses when active and how they respond to their environment, and you'll increase your bass angling success!

(BSL7) TROPHY BASS - If you're more interested in wrestling with one or two monster largemouth than with a "panful" of yearlings, then learn what techniques and locations will improve your chances.

> ### TWO TROPHIES!
> *"By using your techniques and reading your Bass Series Library of books, I was able to catch the two biggest bass I've ever caught!"*
> B. Conley, Cromwell, IN

(BSL8) ANGLER'S GUIDE TO BASS PATTERNS - Catch bass every time out by learning how to develop a productive pattern quickly and effectively. "Bass Patterns" is a reference source for all anglers, regardless of where they live or their skill level. Learn how to choose the right lure, presentation and habitat under various weather and environmental conditions!

(BSL9) BASS GUIDE TIPS - Learn secret techniques known only in a certain region or state that often work in waters all around the country. It's this new approach that usually results in excellent bass angling success. Learn how to apply what the country's top guides know!

Nine Great Volumes To Help You Catch More and Larger Bass!

(LB1) LARRY LARSEN ON BASS TACTICS

is the ultimate "how-to" book that focuses on proven productive methods. Hundreds of highlighted tips and drawings in our LARSEN ON BASS SERIES explain how you

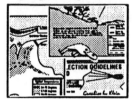

can catch more and larger bass in waters all around the country. This reference source by America's best known bass fishing writer will be invaluable to both the avid novice and expert angler!

BEST EVER!

"Just finished Bass Tactics and thought it was your best yet! I particularly liked the topographic illustrations."
R. Knight, San Angelo, TX

(PF1) PEACOCK BASS EXPLOSIONS! by Larry Larsen

A must read for those anglers who are interested in catching the world's most exciting fresh water fish! Detailed tips, trip planning and tactics for peacocks in South Florida, Venezuela, Brazil, Puerto Rico, Hawaii and other destinations. This book explores the most effective tactics to take the aggressive peacock bass. You'll learn how to catch

more and larger fish using the valuable information from the author and expert angler, a four-time peacock bass world-record holder. It's the first comprehensive discussion on this wild and colorful fish.

BASS WATERS GUIDE SERIES by Larry Larsen

The most productive bass waters are described in this multi-volume series, including boat ramps, seasonal tactics, water characteristics and more. Numerous maps and photos detail specific locations.

SEND ANOTHER ONE!

"Received Central Florida Bass Waters. It's great! Send me South Florida!" D.Eimers, Naples, FL

(BW1) GUIDE TO NORTH FLORIDA BASS WATERS - Covers from Orange Lake north and west. Includes Lakes Lochloosa, Talquin and Seminole, the St. Johns, Nassau, Suwannee and Apalachicola Rivers; Newnans Lake, St. Mary's River, Juniper Lake, Ortega River, Lake Jackson, Deer Point Lake, Panhandle Mill Ponds and many more!

(BW2) GUIDE TO CENTRAL FLORIDA BASS WATERS - Covers from Tampa/Orlando to Palatka. Includes Lakes George, Rodman, Monroe, Tarpon and the Harris Chain, the St. Johns, Oklawaha and Withlacoochee Rivers, the Ocala Forest, Crystal River, Hillsborough River, Conway Chain, Homosassa River,

TATTERED BOOKS!

"The Bass Waters Series are as great as the rest of your bass books. I must have read the Central Florida book 50 times!"
R. Michalski, Meridien, CT

Lake Minneola, Lake Weir, Lake Hart, Spring Runs and many more!

(BW3) GUIDE TO SOUTH FLORIDA BASS WATERS - Covers from I-4 to the Everglades. Includes Lakes Tohopekaliga, Kissimmee, Okeechobee, Poinsett, Tenoroc and Blue Cypress, the Winter Haven Chain, Fellsmere Farm 13. Caloosahatchee River, Lake June-in-Winter, the Everglades, Lake Istokpoga, Peace River, Crooked Lake, Lake Osborne, St. Lucie Canal, Shell Creek, Lake Marian, Lake Pierce, Webb Lake and many more!

OUTDOOR TRAVEL SERIES
by Larry Larsen and M. Timothy O'Keefe

Candid guides on the best charters, time of the year, and other recommendations that can make your next fishing and/or diving trip much more enjoyable.

(OT1) FISH & DIVE THE CARIBBEAN - Vol. 1 Northern Caribbean, including Cozumel, Cayman Islands, Bahamas, Jamaica, Virgin Islands. Required reading for fishing and diving enthusiasts who want to know the most cost-effective means to enjoy these and other Caribbean islands.

(OT3) FISH & DIVE FLORIDA & The Keys - Where and how to plan a vacation to America's most popular fishing and diving destination. Features include artificial reef loran numbers; freshwater springs/caves; coral reefs/barrier islands; gulf stream/passes; inshore flats/channels; and back country estuaries.

> **BEST BOOK CONTENT!**
> *"Fish &Dive the Caribbean" was a finalist in the Best Book Content Category of the National Association of Independent Publishers (NAIP). Over 500 books were submitted by publishers including Simon & Schuster and Turner Publishing. Said the judges "An excellent source book with invaluable instructions. Written by two nationally-known experts who, indeed, know what vacationing can be!"*

DIVING SERIES by M. Timothy O'Keefe

(DL1) DIVING TO ADVENTURE shows how to get started in underwater photography, how to use current to your advantage, how to avoid seasickness, how to dive safely after dark, and how to plan a dive vacation, including live-aboard diving.

(DL2) MANATEES- OUR VANISHING MERMAIDS is an in-depth overview of nature's strangest-looking, gentlest animals. They're among America's most endangered mammals. The book covers where to see manatees while diving, why they may be living fossils, their unique life cycle, and much more.

UNCLE HOMER'S OUTDOOR CHUCKLE BOOK
by Homer Circle, Fishing Editor, Sports Afield

(OC1) In his inimitable humorous style, "Uncle Homer" relates jokes, tales, personal anecdotes and experiences covering several decades in the outdoors. These stories, memories and moments will bring grins, chuckles and deep down belly laughs as you wend your way through the folksy copy and cartoons. If you appreciate the lighter side of life, this book is a must!

OUTDOOR ADVENTURE LIBRARY
by Vin T. Sparano, Editor-in-Chief, Outdoor Life

(OA1) HUNTING DANGEROUS GAME - Live the adventure of hunting those dangerous animals that hunt back! Track a rogue elephant, survive a grizzly attack, and face a charging Cape buffalo. These classic tales will make you very nervous next time you're in the woods!

> **KEEP ME UPDATED!**
> *"I would like to get on your mailing list. I really enjoy your books!"*
> G. Granger, Cypress, CA

(OA2) GAME BIRDS & GUN DOGS - A unique collection of tales about hunters, their dogs and the upland game and waterfowl they hunt. You will read about good gun dogs and heart-breaking dogs, but never about bad dogs, because there's no such animal.

COASTAL FISHING GUIDES
by Frank Sargeant

A unique "where-to" series of detailed secret spots for Florida's finest saltwater fishing. These guide books describe hundreds of little-known honeyholes and exactly how to fish them. Prime seasons, baits and lures, marinas and dozens of detailed maps of the prime spots are included. The comprehensive index helps the reader to further pinpoint productive areas and tactics. Over $160 worth of personally-marked NOAA charts in the two books.

> **EXCELLENT PUBLICATIONS!**
> *"I would like to commend Frank on his excellent saltwater fishing series. I own them all and have read each of them three or four times!"*
> W. La Piedra, Cape Coral, FL

(FG1) FRANK SARGEANT'S SECRET SPOTS Tampa Bay to Cedar Key Covers Hillsborough River and Davis Island through the Manatee River, Mullet Key and the Suwannee River.

(FG2) FRANK SARGEANT'S SECRET SPOTS Southwest Florida Covers from Sarasota Bay to Marco.

INSHORE SERIES
by Frank Sargeant

(IL1) THE SNOOK BOOK-"Must" reading for anyone who loves the pursuit of this unique sub-tropic species. Every aspect of how you can find and catch big snook is covered, in all seasons and all waters where snook are found.

(IL2) THE REDFISH BOOK-Packed with expertise from the nation's leading redfish anglers and guides, this book covers every aspect of finding and fooling giant reds. You'll learn secret techniques revealed for the first time. After reading this informative book, you'll catch more redfish on your next trip!

(IL3) THE TARPON BOOK-Find and catch the wily "silver king" along the Gulf Coast, north through the mid-Atlantic, and south along Central and South American coastlines. Numerous experts share their most productive techniques.

(IL4) THE TROUT BOOK-Jammed with tips from the nation's leading trout guides and light tackle anglers. For both the old salt and the rank amateur who pursue the spotted weakfish, or seatrout, throughout the coastal waters of the Gulf and Atlantic.

> **SEND ME MORE!**
> *"I am delighted with Frank Sargeant's Redfish Book. Please let me know when others in the Inshore Series will be available."*
> J.A'Hern, Columbia, S.C.
>
> **GIFT ORDER!**
> *"I have three of your Inshore Series books. My daughter just moved to Homosassa from Michigan and I want to send her the same books!."*
> N. Pappas, Bonita Springs, FL
>
> **PERSONALIZED PAK!**
> *"Thanks for the catalog. I would like to order your four-book autographed set on inshore fishing."*
> L.Jones, LakeWorth, FL

HUNTING LIBRARY
by John E. Phillips

(DH1) MASTERS' SECRETS OF DEER HUNTING - Increase your deer hunting success by learning from the masters of the sport. New information on tactics and strategies is included in this book, the most comprehensive of its kind.

(DH2) THE SCIENCE OF DEER HUNTING Covers why, where and when a deer moves and deer behavior. Find the answers to many of the toughest deer hunting problems a sportsman ever encounters!

(DH3) MASTERS' SECRETS OF BOW-HUNTING DEER - Learn the skills required to take more bucks with a bow, even during gun season. A must read for those who walk into the woods with a strong bow and a swift shaft.

(TH1) MASTERS' SECRETS OF TURKEY HUNTING - Masters of the sport have solved some of the most difficult problems you can encounter while hunting wily longbeards with bows, blackpowder guns and shotguns. Learn the 10 deadly sins of turkey hunting.

> **RECOMMENDATION!**
> *"Masters' Secrets of Turkey Hunting is one of the best books around. If you're looking for a good turkey book, buy it!"*
> J. Spencer, Stuttgart Daily Leader, AR
>
> **NO BRAGGIN'!**
> *"From anyone else Masters' Secrets of Deer Hunting would be bragging and unbelievable. But not with John Phillips, he's paid his dues!"* F. Snare, Brookville Star, OH

(BP1) BLACKPOWDER HUNTING SECRETS - Learn how to take more game during and after the season with black powder guns. If you've been hunting with black powder for years, this book will teach you better tactics to use throughout the year.

FISHING LIBRARY

(CF1) MASTERS' SECRETS OF CRAPPIE FISHING by John E. Phillips Learn how to make crappie start biting again once they have stopped, select the best jig color, find crappie in a cold front, through the ice, or in 100-degree heat. Unusual, productive crappie fishing techniques are included.

(CF2) CRAPPIE TACTICS by Larry Larsen - Whether you are a beginner or a seasoned crappie fisherman, this book will improve your catch! The book includes some basics for fun fishing, advanced techniques for year 'round crappie and tournament preparation.

> **CRAPPIE COUP!**
> *"After reading your crappie book, I'm ready to overthrow the 'crappie king' at my lakeside housing development!"*
> R. Knorr, Haines City, FL

(CF3) MASTERS' SECRETS OF CATFISHING by John E. Phillips is your best guide to catching the best-tasting, elusive cats. If you want to know the best time of the year, the most productive places and which states to fish in your pursuit of Mr. Whiskers, then this book is for you. Special features include how to find and take monster cats, what baits to use and when, how to find a tailrace groove and more strategies for rivers or lakes.

INDEX

About Our Cover Painting

The beautiful painting of the seven peacock bass (species and color variations) on our cover is by renown marine watercolorist, Beverly Thomas. Her speciality is marine watercolors with collage. For the extremely facile Florida artist, this would seem to be a natural subject matter. She is a third generation Floridian whose father and grandparents were all commercial fishermen and charter boatmen.

Thomas herself is a high school art teacher in Coconut Creek, Florida. Her work has won multiple awards at various art festivals around the country. An environmentalist at heart, Thomas is avidly committed to painting marine creatures and to conserving them. The artist believes it is much better to commission a painting of a trophy than to destroy it.

For information on her sensitive and telling interpretations of many wild creatures, Thomas can be contacted at 2831 NE 11 Terrace, Pompano Beach, FL 33064 or by phoning (305) 781-3147.

Limited Edition Prints Available

Limited Edition Prints of our beautiful back cover painting by Beverly Thomas in its original size of 11" by 11" are available from Larsen's Outdoor Publishing. Individually numbered and personally signed by the artist with the title "Peacock Bass", the shrink-wrapped, foam-core-mounted prints are only $40.00 while quantities last. This collector's item is suitable for framing and makes a handsome addition to any room in the house or office.

#LEP-1 ... $40.00

Quality "Peacock Bass Explosions" T-Shirts

We also have available all-cotton T-Shirts that feature the beautiful back cover painting. Entitled "Peacock Bass Explosions", these quality white shirts with art on their front can be ordered in sizes M, Lg, or XL. They are priced at only $15.00. Please specify size when ordering.   #TS-1 ... $15.00

Breinigsville, PA USA
25 June 2010
240551BV00003B/2/P